ITALY TRAVEL GUIDE 2023 CORTONA

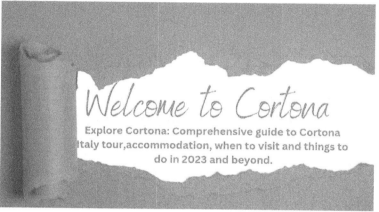

Welcome to Cortona

Explore Cortona: Comprehensive guide to Cortona Italy tour, accommodation, when to visit and things to do in 2023 and beyond.

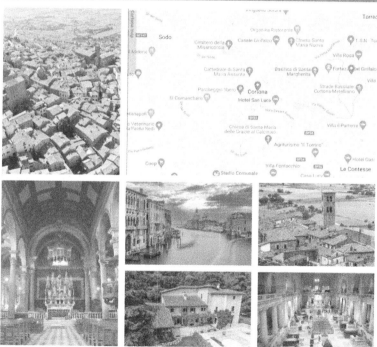

JENNIFER C. WEBBER

Copyright © [Jennifer C. Webber] [2023]

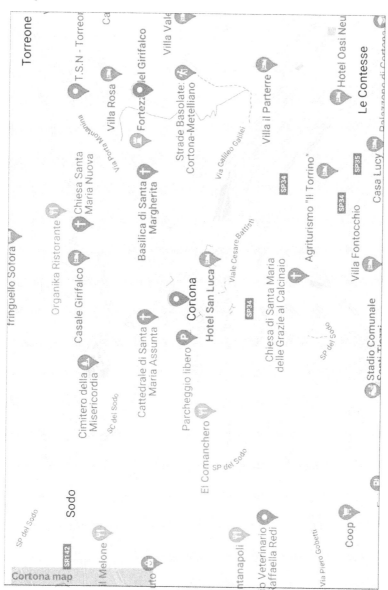

TABLE OF CONTENT

INTRODUCTION

Welcome to Cortona, a charming Italian town tucked away in Tuscany. Every traveler who is fortunate enough to visit this charming hilltop town will have an amazing experience as it readily captures the essence of Italian charm. Cortona is a place has it all, offering a rich history, stunning scenery, and a thriving cultural life.

You'll experience a sense of time travel as you stroll through the quaint cobblestone alleys dotted with historic stone homes decorated with colorful flowers. The town is a great trove for archaeologists because its history can be traced back to the Etruscans. With panoramic views of the neighboring valleys, vineyards, and olive groves provided by its advantageous hilltop location, it is in a picture-perfect setting at every turn.

The ancient town of Cortona is a charming maze of medieval structures, churches, and piazzas, each with a unique tale to tell. Piazza della Repubblica, the town's central square, is where residents and guests alike go to enjoy cappuccino, engage in vibrant discussion, and bask in the warm Tuscan sun. You may find quaint boutiques, artisan stores, and trattorias that serve delectable Tuscan fare all around the Piazza.

Cortona is a treasure trove for art lovers as the city has a distinguished cultural history. A magnificent collection of Renaissance artwork, including pieces by Fra Angelico and Luca Signorelli, is kept in the eminent Museo Diocesano.

It's impossible to describe how breathtaking the latter's paintings in the Cappella del Tabernacolo are; they transport you to a world of minute details and moving storytelling.

Cortona offers a wonderful setting to explore for those who enjoy the outdoors. Take a leisurely trek across the gently undulating hills or a bike ride along the charming backroads. Wineries and olive orchards beautify the surrounding landscape, luring you to sample the local cuisine. Don't pass up the chance to visit a nearby winery where you can indulge in wine samples and learn the techniques used to produce the famed Tuscan wines.

Throughout the year, Cortona organizes a diverse calendar of events and festivals in addition to its historic charm and natural beauty. There is always something going on to engage and excite visitors, from the exciting Giostra dell'Archidado, a medieval jousting event, to the Cortona Mix Festival, which honors art, music, and culture.

Cortona provides a wide range of activities that will make an enduring impression on your heart, whether you're looking for a tranquil retreat, a cultural voyage, or a culinary tour. As we explore the undiscovered attractions, insider knowledge, and unique customs that make Cortona such an exceptional location, this travel guide will be your dependable travel companion. So prepare to explore this time-honored town's mysteries as you pack your luggage and bask in the warmth of Tuscan hospitality. Your Cortona journey is waiting!

Culture and History

Explore the amazing fabric of history and culture that runs through Cortona's historic streets. This timeless town has a colorful history that dates back to the far-off Etruscan era and has left a lasting impression on its cobblestone streets and important historical sites.

Cortona rose to prominence as Curtun, one of the most important Etruscan city-states, around 600 BCE. Cortona's foundation was laid by the ancient Etruscan civilization, which is known for its creative and architectural prowess.

Impressive traces of their presence may still be seen today. You may still see remnants of this prehistoric society if you take a stroll around the town's streets, such as the Etruscan walls that ring it and serve as a reminder of Cortona's earliest days.

The Romans took control of Cortona in the fourth century BCE, beginning a new age of cultural impact. The town prospered as a significant agricultural and trade hub during Roman administration. The Roman Theater, which still stands today as a testament of Cortona's splendor during this era, is just one of the remarkable structures the Romans built that left their mark.

Cortona saw numerous changes in the balance of power and influences over the ages. It developed into a thriving medieval fortress throughout the Middle Ages, when competing aristocratic families fought for dominance. The town saw the rise and fall of feudal lords, the widening of its city walls, and the building of opulent churches and palaces that now stand as architectural landmarks.

The great artist Luca Signorelli, who was born in Cortona in 1441, is an important character in that city's history. The beautiful frescoes by Signorelli that may be found in the Cappella del Tabernacolo are a lasting testament to his artistic prowess. These masterpieces, which were painted between 1517 and 1519, represent scenes from the Apocalypse and the Last Judgment and display the artist's amazing skill and compelling storytelling.

The birth of renowned Baroque painter and architect Pietro da Cortona in the year 1722 was a crucial turning point in Cortona's history. With his opulent frescoes and architectural creations, Pietro da Cortona, also known by his birth name Pietro Berrettini, made an everlasting impression on the art world. His contributions to the community's creative history are visible in the wonderful frescoes he painted on the walls of the Church of Santa Maria delle Grazie al Calcinaio.

Cortona is still a thriving center for culture and the arts today. Its streets are bustling with art galleries, workshops, and boutiques where you can see how the inventiveness of modern artists blends with the echoes of the past. The town's passion for the arts is celebrated through a variety of events and exhibitions, luring visitors from all over the world to experience its lively environment.

You'll experience the past as a living tapestry as you explore Cortona's historical and cultural treasures. The town's history is a captivating voyage through time, starting with its early Etruscan origins and ending with the breathtaking artwork of Luca Signorelli and Pietro da Cortona. Embrace Cortona's character, where the past and present coexist together to provide an experience that goes beyond simple tourism and brings you closer to the heart of this wonderful place.

Geography and Climate

Cortona is fortunate to have a landscape that is both gorgeous and diversified. The town's hilltop location provides panoramic views of lush valleys, rolling hills, and miles upon miles of vineyards and olive groves, creating a captivating background.

Cortona is conveniently situated in the center of Italy, making it simple to reach from important cities like Florence, Siena, and Rome. In addition to offering breathtaking views, its high location also exudes peace and remoteness from the rush of modern life.

The town's mild climate is a result of its height, which is roughly 600 meters (1,970 feet) above sea level. The average summertime temperature of Cortona ranges from 77°F to 86°F, or 25°C to 30°C.

The warm weather encourages outdoor activities like wandering around the streets, hiking in the nearby hills, and enjoying the Tuscan countryside. The coolness of the evenings is ideal for a leisurely meal in one of Cortona's exquisite outdoor trattorias.

As the leaves on the vineyards and forests change into a rich palette of reds, oranges, and yellows, autumn in Cortona reveals a tapestry of brilliant colors. With temperatures steadily dropping to between 15°C and 25°C (59°F and 77°F), it's the perfect time for wine tastings and lovely walks through the changing leaves.

Cortona is endowed with a serene beauty in the winter as the town enjoys a tranquil atmosphere. Although lows of about 5° to 10°C (41° to 50°F) are possible, the moderate winters rarely experience bitterly cold temperatures or significant snowfall. The calm streets make for the ideal environment for relaxing at a café, visiting museums, or soaking up the warmth of the community.

Cortona comes to life as spring awakens with beautiful flowers and lush surroundings. A gradual increase in temperature from 15°C to 20°C (59°F to 68°F) encourages visitors to enjoy the outdoors and observe the revitalization of the town. The spring is the best season to visit Cortona's surroundings, go on wine tours, and take in the abundant natural beauty.

The terrain of Cortona also favors a rich and productive agricultural region. Vineyards that make some of Italy's best wines, such as the renowned Chianti and Vino Nobile di Montepulciano, are adorned in the surrounding hills and valleys. Contrarily, the olive orchards produce the highly sought-after extra virgin olive oil, a staple of Tuscan cooking.

In essence, Cortona's geology and environment weave a beautiful tapestry of rolling hills, olive groves, and vineyards into a region with warm weather all year round.

Cortona's natural beauty and welcoming environment make it the perfect setting for your Tuscan trip, whether you visit during the summer's sunny days or the quiet stillness of winter.

Reasons to visit Cortona

Travelers are drawn to Cortona by its enduring attractiveness and irresistible charm because it captures the very spirit of Italy. There are many compelling reasons to discover this charming Tuscan town, from its rich history and cultural legacy to its breathtaking views and kind friendliness.

Cortona is home to several historic wonders that history buffs will adore. Discover relics of the Etruscan culture, which flourished here thousands of years ago, as you meander through its meandering alleyways. Discover the town's surrounding Etruscan walls, which are evidence of Cortona's past as a thriving city-state. Experience the creative history of well-known artists like Luca Signorelli and Pietro da Cortona, whose masterpieces adorn the town's churches and museums and will take you to a world of brilliant creativity.

The alluring terrain and beautiful scenery of Cortona are a visual and emotional feast. The village, which is perched on a hill, provides breathtaking panoramic views of rolling hills, vineyards, and olive groves as far as the eye can see. Cortona's natural beauty will astound you whether you prefer to hike through the nearby countryside, bike along gorgeous paths, or simply take in the beauty of the Tuscan countryside.

Cortona welcomes visitors to immerse themselves in its dynamic cultural environment in addition to its history and natural beauty. Investigate the crowded piazzas where people and tourists mix and enjoy the pace of Italian life. Explore artisanal studios, galleries, and shops that highlight the region's ingenuity and workmanship. Enjoy the flavors of Tuscan cuisine, which features seasonal ingredients and age-old recipes that have been refined.

The town of Cortona is alive all year long thanks to the numerous events and festivals that fill its calendar. There is always something going on to pique your senses and immerse you in the dynamic atmosphere of Cortona, from medieval jousting tournaments and processions that recreate ancient traditions to music festivals that honor the arts.

Every area of Cortona is infused with the warm hospitality of the Tuscany, making visitors feel like valued guests. Talk to the residents informally; they are happy to tell you about their hometown's history and customs. The inhabitants of Cortona will make you feel welcomed and accepted, whether you need advice on where to eat, suggestions for off-the-beaten-path sights, or simply a warm grin.

An invitation to experience Tuscany's ageless beauty and genuine charm is extended to you when you travel to Cortona. Every part of Cortona entices you to set out on a journey of discovery and make experiences that will last a lifetime, from its compelling history and rich cultural legacy to its stunning scenery and kind hospitality. Allow yourself to be enchanted by the allure of this wonderful place as Cortona works its magic all around you.

CHAPTER 1

Traveling to Cortona is an exciting adventure that needs to be well planned in order to be effortless and unforgettable. Making the most of your trip to this charming Tuscan town requires careful planning, from choosing when to go to scheduling transportation and lodging.

It's important to visit Cortona at the proper time of year because each one offers a different atmosphere and assortment of activities. Think about which season you enjoy more: the vivacious energy of summer, the alluring colors of autumn, the warm atmosphere of winter, or the burgeoning beauty of spring. To choose the best time that fits your choices, consider your interests and desired experiences.

With careful planning and close attention to detail, you can create the perfect environment for an amazing journey on your vacation to Cortona. Prepare to set out on an astonishing journey as Cortona's power is revealed to you.

The Best Time to Go

The decision of when to travel to Cortona is a lovely conundrum because this Tuscan town provides distinctive experiences and charming activities all year long. You can personalize your trip according to your preferences and interests because each season has its own beauty. You should take into account the highlights and festival dates below when choosing the best time to book your vacation.

Spring(March to May)

- A lovely time to visit Cortona is in the spring, from March to May. When nature rises, the surrounding landscapes are painted in vivid hues. The town is ideal for outdoor exploration because of its warm climate, which ranges from 15°C to 20°C (59°F to 68°F). You can participate in the Easter festivities in April by taking part in the customary processions and religious rituals that give the streets a solemn mood.

Summer (June through August)

- From June through August, Cortona experiences a summer season marked by long, sunny days and a buzzing vitality. With an average temperature range of 25°C to 30°C (77°F to 86°F), outdoor activities are delightfully enjoyable. A wide range of cultural activities are also available during the summer, including the Cortona Mix Festival, a multidisciplinary event that combines music, art, and literature. The festival, which takes place in July and draws well-known worldwide performers, provides a rich and varied experience.

Fall (September through November)

- Cortona is blessed with spectacular scenery during the autumn months of September to November when the foliage turns into a tapestry of reds, oranges, and yellows. With temperatures ranging from 15°C to 25°C (59°F to 77°F), the weather is quite pleasant. At the Cortona On The Move photography festival, which takes place in September, the town transforms into a gallery, displaying potent visual narratives from renowned photographers from around the world.

Winter (December to February)

From December through February, Cortona's winter season welcomes you into a warm and welcoming environment. Despite a temperature range of 5°C to 10°C (41°F to 50°F), the moderate winters rarely have bitterly cold temperatures or significant snowfall. The town is decorated for Christmas, and the inhabitants join together to celebrate with customary occasions like the Cortona Antiquaria market, where antique enthusiasts can peruse a broad variety of treasures.

Cortona organizes a variety of events and festivals all year long that contribute to the town's vibrant cultural life. The August Tuscan Sun Festival, which blends music, art, and cuisine, draws well-known performers from around the world and culminates in memorable performances. The Archidado Joust, a medieval competition where competitors fight in archery matches while clothed historically, takes place in September and will instantly transport you to the Middle Ages.

Check the precise dates and hours of these events and festivals when making travel plans, as they may change from year to year. Including these activities in your itinerary will give your trip to Cortona a special local touch and enable you to thoroughly immerse yourself in the lively cultural scene of the town.

No matter when you decide to travel to Cortona, its enduring beauty and gracious welcome will steal your heart. Take advantage of the opportunity to participate in the lively celebrations of the town and embrace the charm of each season to make lifelong memories.

Understanding the visa procedures and criteria before traveling to Cortona, Italy, will help to secure a simple admission into the nation. Your nationality and the length of your stay will determine the precise visa requirements. Here is a general description of the Cortona visa requirements.

Find out first if you require a visa to enter Italy. European Union (EU) and Schengen Area nationals can stay in Italy for up to 90 days during a 180-day span without needing a visa. However, you will normally need to apply for a visa if you are a citizen of a non-EU or non-Schengen nation.

Contact the closest Italian embassy or consulate in your own country to start the visa application process. For your particular visa type, they will give you the information and a list of needed documents. Typically, you'll need to provide your passport, a filled out application form, proof of travel plans (such as tickets and lodging information), financial documentation showing you have the means to support your stay, proof of travel insurance, and a recent passport-sized photo.

It is crucial to give yourself enough time to process your visa because it varies based on the consulate and the season. To guarantee prompt processing, it is advised to submit your application at least three months before your anticipated travel dates. Due to the anticipated high amount of applications, it is advised to apply even early during popular travel times, such as the summer.

The kind and length of the visa you're asking for affect the visa fees as well. According to my knowledge, a short-term Schengen visa costs €80 for adults and €40 for kids between the ages of 6 and 12. Please be aware, though, that visa fees might fluctuate, so you should double-check them when you submit your application.

Send your application to the Italian embassy or consulate once you have obtained all necessary documentation. Your application and any supporting materials will be examined by them. They will let you know if more information or an interview are required. You will receive a visa sticker for your passport after being accepted, enabling you to enter Italy and travel to Cortona.

During your visit to Cortona, it is imperative that you adhere to the terms of your visa. Make careful that your visit does not last longer than the time period permitted by your visa because doing so may result in penalties or other legal repercussions.

The official website of the Italian embassy or consulate in your country should be consulted for the most up-to-date and accurate information regarding visa requirements, processing procedures, and charges. Please be aware that visa requirements and procedures can change over time.

You may travel to Cortona with confidence and be prepared to enjoy all that this alluring Tuscan town has to offer by being aware of the visa requirements and going through the proper channels.

To ensure a hassle-free financial experience when visiting Cortona, Italy, it is crucial to become familiar with the local currency and comprehend financial problems. Here is some useful information to assist you in navigating Cortona's currency exchange, payment options, and other financial considerations.

Italy uses the Euro (EUR) as its official currency. Including Cortona, it is widely acknowledged across the entire nation. To guarantee you have local money for your expenses, it is important to exchange your cash to Euros before your trip or upon arrival in Italy.

Banks, post offices, and currency exchange offices are just a few places where you can find exchange services. A few larger hotels may also provide currency exchange services, albeit they might charge more or offer worse exchange rates. To select the most advantageous choice, it is advised to evaluate exchange rates and expenses. When exchanging money, keep in mind to include a legitimate form of identification, such as your passport.

Bank cards

Bank cards are welcomed freely in Cortona, particularly in lodgings, dining establishments, and major stores. The most widely used credit cards are Visa and Mastercard, with American Express and Diners Club possibly having a smaller acceptance range. To prevent any potential problems with card usage, it is advised to let your credit card company know ahead of time about your travel intentions to Italy. Recognize that certain smaller companies or family-run enterprises might only accept cash; it is advised to carry some Euros just in case.

ATMs

They are commonly accessible in Cortona and are known as "Bancomat" in Italian. They can be located at significant transportation hubs, close to commercial districts, and in banks. Using your debit or credit card, ATMs make it simple to get cash in euros. It is wise to ask your bank about any fees or withdrawal restrictions that could be in place.

In restaurants, cafes, and bars, it is common to give a small tip for the wait staff. Although a service charge is frequently included in the bill, it is customary to round it up or contribute an extra 5–10% as a sign of gratitude for excellent service. Although not required, tipping hotel staff members like the concierge or housekeepers is also appreciated. It's crucial to remember that tipping customs might differ and that it ultimately depends on you.

While exploring Cortona, it is suggested to keep your cash and belongings locked up. Put your money, cards, and important papers in hotel safes or safe pockets. Avoid flashing big quantities of cash in public and be on the lookout for pickpockets in crowded places.

To avoid any problems using your card or potential fraud warnings, it's crucial to let your bank or credit card issuer know about your vacation plans. Ask them about any international transaction fees that might be associated with using your card in Italy.

You may conduct financial transactions in Cortona with ease by being aware of the local currency and financial issues, which will make your trip to this alluring Tuscan town worry-free.

Communication and Language

To guarantee a seamless and pleasurable experience, it's beneficial to take language and communication considerations into account while arranging a vacation to Cortona, Italy. Here are some helpful tidbits to help you overcome language challenges and support successful conversation while you're there.

Italian is the predominant language used in Cortona and is also the official language of Italy. Even though English is frequently spoken and understood in tourist regions, learning a few fundamental Italian greetings and phrases is always helpful. The effort is valued by the locals, and it might improve your encounters and cultural immersion. A cordial connection can be created with a few simple salutations like "buongiorno" (good morning), "buonasera" (good evening), and "grazie" (thank you).

Many signage, menus, and tourist information are available in both Italian and English in Cortona. However, you might run into fewer English speakers if you visit smaller businesses or venture off the usual road. To help with communication in these circumstances, it can be useful to have a small phrasebook or have a translation program on your smartphone.

Don't be afraid to contact the Cortona tourist information offices if you need help or have special questions. The personnel there speaks several languages, including English, and can give you useful information, directions, and maps. They can answer your questions about directions, suggestions, and other travel-related issues.

You might see solely Italian-written menus when dining out in Cortona. Accept the chance to sample genuine regional food, and don't be hesitant to ask the server for advice or an explanation of the dishes. When it comes to establishing effective communication and receiving first-rate service, politeness and friendliness go a long way.

It's important to note that in Italian culture, nonverbal communication is quite important. Italians are expressive people who express themselves through hand gestures and facial expressions. Understanding and interacting with the locals can be improved by observing and adjusting to these nonverbal signs.

You can move around Cortona with ease and interact with the local culture in a meaningful way by being aware of language and communication considerations. Take advantage of the chance to learn a few fundamental Italian phrases, use translation tools as necessary, and approach contacts with a polite and courteous demeanor. The ability to communicate effectively builds relationships, improves your vacation experience, and enables you to fully appreciate Cortona's beauty and allure.

Permit to Stay

To guarantee a lawful and trouble-free stay in the nation, it's critical to be informed of the conditions for stay permits. Here are some useful details on stay authorizations for your travel preparations.

You can stay in Italy, including Cortona, for up to 90 days during a 180-day period if you are a citizen of the European Union (EU) or the Schengen Area. Short-term trips and pleasure travel are made possible by this.

However, if your intended stay in Cortona is longer than 90 days and you are a non-EU or non-Schengen citizen, you must apply for a stay permit, commonly known as a "permesso di soggiorno," within eight days of your arrival in Italy.

There are various steps in the application procedure for a stay permission. The first step is to make an appointment at the regional police office, also known as "Questura" or "Ufficio Immigrazione," which is often the largest city in the province where you will be staying.

You must bring the necessary paperwork to your appointment, which includes a completed application form, a current passport, proof of lodging in Cortona, evidence of sufficient funds to cover your stay, proof of health insurance coverage, and any other documentation the authorities may require.

You can also be asked to submit to a medical examination and supply biometric information like your fingerprints. Your application will be processed by the authorities, and if accepted, you will be given a temporary stay permission that is effective up until the issuance of the permanent permit.

It's crucial to remember that the application process for a stay permit can be difficult and time-consuming. For thorough instructions and precise requirements, it is advised to contact an immigration attorney or visit the local police department's official website.

Once you have gotten your stay permission, it is very important to keep it on you at all times when visiting Cortona as you can be asked to show it by the authorities.

It is advised to speak with the relevant Italian authorities or seek legal counsel if you intend to carry out activities in

Cortona like job, study, or long-term living in order to comprehend the precise needs and procedures for getting the necessary permissions or visas.

You may guarantee a legitimate and compliant stay in Cortona by being informed of the requirements for stay permits and carrying out the relevant steps. It's crucial to be well-informed and organized so that you may completely enjoy your visit in this picturesque Tuscan town without encountering any unneeded difficulties.

CHAPTER 2

Greetings from Cortona! For tourists looking for the ideal fusion of history, culture, and magnificent views, this quaint hilltop village in Tuscany offers a lovely vacation. The journey to Cortona is an adventure in and of itself, with a variety of modes of transportation that let you take in the splendor of the Italian landscape en route.

The main international airports in Rome and Florence are the most popular entry points if you're traveling from overseas. Both airports provide straightforward connections to Cortona, making it simple to begin your Tuscan vacation.

By Air

There are a few important points to bear in mind for a trouble-free flight if you're going to travel to Cortona by air. To help you with your travel planning, the information about the closest airports, airline prices, departure and arrival times, travel distance, and contact information is provided below.

Rome Fiumicino Airport (Leonardo da Vinci Airport) and Florence Airport (Amerigo Vespucci Airport) are the two main airports that offer easy access to Cortona.

Rome, Fiumicino Airport.

Address:

Via dell'Aeroporto di Fiumicino, 320, 00054 Italy's Fiumicino RM, Italy

Flight Price: Flight prices can change based on where you travel from and the season. For the most recent costs, it is advisable to check with several airlines and travel websites.

Website: www.viator.com/rome-tourism

or www.adr.it/fiumicino

phone: +390665951

Time of Departure: Depending on the airline and the flight itinerary, departure times vary. For departure timings, check the airline's website or contact your travel agent.

Arrival time: From Rome Fiumicino Airport to Cortona, the flight should take between two and three hours. Depending on the flight you choose, arrival times will change.

Distance covered: There are about 220 kilometers between Rome Fiumicino Airport and Cortona.

Florence Airport

Address: Via del Termine, 11, 50127 Firenze FI, Italy

Flight Price: It vary just like that of Rome Fiumicino Airport

Website: www.airport-florence.com or www.aeroporto.firenze.it

Phone: +3905530615

Departure Time: Depending on the airline and the flight schedule, departure times change. For departure timings, consult the airline's website or your travel agent.

Arrival Time: The flight from Florence Airport to Cortona is anticipated to take about 1.5 hours. The flight you choose will determine your arrival time.

Distance Covered: Cortona and Florence Airport are around 125 kilometers apart, roughly.

It's crucial to remember that travel prices, schedules, and arrival times can change based on the time of year and airline availability. For the most precise and recent information, it is advised to verify with airlines and travel companies. Additionally, to get the best offers and availability, think about booking your flights far in advance.

You can continue traveling to Cortona after landing at either the Rome Fiumicino Airport or the Florence Airport by taking advantage of the numerous modes of transportation offered, including train services, personal transports, or rented cars. You may easily get to Cortona using these choices and start exploring its fascinating history, cultural treasures, and stunning scenery.

By Train

One common method of transportation to Cortona is via plane, and from the closest airport, you may easily proceed to Cortona by train. The main train station for getting to Cortona is Camucia-Cortona, which provides easy connections from a number of Italian cities. You may learn everything you need to know here:

Camucia-Cortona Train Station

Address: Piazza Stazione, 3 in Camucia, Cortona (AR), Italy, 52044.

Cost of Train: Depending on where you depart from, train tickets to Camucia-Cortona range in price. For precise pricing information, it is advised to verify with the relevant railway operators or websites

1. From Milan to Cortona

www.omio.com

2. From Pietrasanta to Cortona

www.rome2rio.com

Phone: +390668475475

Departure Time

Trains depart from Camucia-Cortona at regular intervals throughout the day, giving passengers flexibility. Depending on the individual train and route you select, departure times will vary.

Arrival Time: Depending on the departure point and the distance traveled by train, Camucia-Cortona arrival time will vary. Checking the train schedules for precise arrival timings is advised.

Distance Covered: Kilometers Traveled: It takes about 200 and 130 kilometers, respectively, to travel to Camucia-Cortona from large cities like Rome and Florence.

The national train operator of Italy has a website at www.trenitalia.com

From Rome's Termini Station, you can catch a train to Camucia-Cortona. The trip provides stunning vistas of the Italian countryside as it travels via picturesque landscapes, vineyards, and quaint towns.

If you're coming from Florence, you can take a train to Camucia-Cortona from Florence's Santa Maria Novella Station. Through undulating hills and olive trees, this path lets you take in the splendor of Tuscany.

It's crucial to remember that the cost of a train ticket can change based on the type of ticket purchased and the type of train (regional, intercity, or high-speed). For the lowest prices and the widest selection of seats, it is important to check the train timetables and purchase your tickets in advance.

You may quickly get to the center of Cortona after arriving at Camucia-Cortona by taking a local bus or a short cab ride. You'll be close to the town's historic core and its enticing attractions, like Piazza della Repubblica and the magnificent Etruscan walls.

You may take advantage of Italy's rail network's ease, comfort, and scenic beauty by choosing the train as your mode of transportation to Cortona. So get on board and allow the train's steady chug to carry you to the alluring world of Cortona.

By Car

For visitors who value the independence and adaptability of the open road, traveling to Cortona by automobile is an excellent choice. You can completely immerse yourself in the grandeur of the Italian countryside by driving through the picturesque landscapes of Tuscany and stopping at lovely towns along the way to take in the stunning vistas. The following information will prepare you for your journey:

Due to the town's numerous access points, Cortona does not have a specific address for driving correspondence. However, you can program your GPS or navigation system to direct you to Cortona's town center or a particular location there.

Cost Price: The price of taking a car to Cortona will vary depending on a number of variables, including the distance you're driving, the cost of gas, any relevant tolls, and parking costs. When organizing your trip, it's a good idea to look up the current fuel rates and take into account any supplemental costs.

Departure Time: Depending on your location and choices, the departure time will vary. It is advised to arrange your departure so that you can reach Cortona in the daytime as this will make traversing the town's winding streets and finding parking easier.

Arrival Time: Depending on your departure point, the flow of traffic, and the route taken, the arrival time may change. It's wise to calculate your arrival time by taking into account the distance to Cortona, the flow of traffic, and any planned detours.

Distance Covered: Depending on where you start and the path you take, you will need to travel a certain amount of miles to get to Cortona. It's between 200 and 130 kilometers away from big cities like Rome and Florence, respectively.

Make sure you have a current driver's license, the required insurance, and an understanding of local driving laws before starting your drive to Cortona. Learn the road signs, parking rules, and any additional limitations that may apply in the places you will be driving through in Italy.

You can enjoy the independence of the roa d and take your time discovering the stunning Tuscan landscape by taking the scenic drive to Cortona. So secure your seatbelt, turn on your preferred soundtrack for the road, and get set to travel to the enchanting village of Cortona and make lifelong memories.

Cortona's transportation choices provide simple methods to go around the city and its surroundings. There are many options to fit your preferences, whether you like exploring on foot, taking public transportation, or hiring a taxi. You may learn everything you need to know about Cortona's transportation options here:

Walking: Cortona is a beautiful town to explore on foot because to its small size and charming streets. Explore hidden nooks, meander through tiny streets, and take in the enchanting ambiance of this historic Etruscan town.

Public transportation: You can get to adjacent cities and attractions from Cortona thanks to the city's effective bus system, which is well connected. Buses are a convenient and affordable kind of transportation that run along predetermined routes. At bus stops and the municipal transportation authority, timetables and route maps are available.

Taxis: Taxis are widely accessible in Cortona and can be a practical option, especially for shorter journeys or when transporting large amounts of stuff. Taxis can be hailed on the street or obtained at authorized stands scattered throughout the town. Before setting out on your trip, it's a good idea to double check the fare with the taxi driver.

Car rental: With a car rental, you may travel at your own pace while discovering Cortona and its surroundings. There are numerous vehicle rental agencies in the area, so you may book one in advance or when you get there. You may easily explore the beautiful Tuscan countryside and go to local sites if you have a car.

Cycling: Enthusiasts can rent bicycles in Cortona and take leisurely rides across the gorgeous rolling hills of Tuscany. Cycling through the countryside provides a distinct viewpoint and enables you to find local treasures.

When selecting a mode of transportation in Cortona, keep in mind things like the distance you intend to travel, your spending limit, and whether you prefer convenience or adventure. Every traveler's needs are catered to in Cortona, whether they like leisurely strolls, public transportation, Taxis, the flexibility of a rental car, or bicycles.

You'll have the chance to immerse yourself in Cortona's rich history, savor the regional food, and take advantage of the welcoming inhabitants as you tour the town and its surrounds. Your trip through Cortona's lovely streets and breathtaking surroundings will be one to remember if you choose the correct mode of transportation.

Chapter 3

This quaint hilltop village provides a wide range of must-see attractions that will enchant you and take you back in time. Here are some of Cortona's must-see landmarks, which range from its magnificent art collections to its well-preserved medieval walls

Cathedral of Cortona

The Duomo, another name for the Cortona Cathedral, stands erect at the town's highest point and welcomes guests with its breathtaking beauty and historical significance. Here is all the information you require about this popular Cortona attraction:

Address: Piazza del Duomo 2, Cortona AR, Italy.

Hours of Operation and Closing:

The Duomo is typically open to visitors from early in the morning until late in the afternoon, though exact hours can change depending on the season. For the most recent information, it is advisable to consult the current timetable or contact the neighborhood tourist information center.

Distance from Cortona:

- The Duomo is conveniently accessible from many locations in Cortona due to its central location. Its prominent location provides panoramic views of the surroundings.

Closest Airport:

- The closest international airport to Cortona is Perugia San Francesco d'Assisi Airport (PEG), which is positioned about 60 kilometers (37 miles) away. Typically, it takes an hour or so to drive from Cortona to the airport in Perugia, depending on traffic.

Closest Train Station:

- The Terontola-Cortona Station, also known as Camucia-Cortona Station, is the one that is most convenient to Cortona. It is situated about 6 kilometers (3.7 miles) from Cortona in the neighbouring hamlet of Camucia. A car or cab will take you from Cortona to Camucia-Cortona Station in around 15 minutes.

It's important to keep in mind that these distances and travel times are only estimates and may change based on the precise route followed and the level of traffic. Before making travel plans, it is always a good idea to check for any updates or changes to available transportation options and schedules.

What to see:

Enter the Duomo to be in awe of its extraordinary architectural and artistic treasures. Take in the exquisite façade that is embellished with elaborate carvings and sculptures. You'll be enthralled by the exquisite paintings, elaborate altar design, and amazing stained glass windows that fill the space with ethereal light inside. Don't pass up the chance to view the beautiful artwork and artifacts that surround this holy place.

What to do:

- Take a moment of solitude on your visit to the Duomo to reflect and take in the atmosphere of this revered location. Visit a Mass or other religious ceremony to encounter the age-old customs and serious ceremonies. Additionally, the Duomo frequently holds concerts and cultural events, giving you a rare chance to fully experience the area's rich artistic past.

How to Tour:

- Consider taking a tour of the Duomo, led by informed locals who may give intriguing insights into the cathedral's history, architecture, and aesthetic significance, to see the cathedral at its fullest. As an alternative, you can take your time and thoroughly enjoy the Duomo's features and atmosphere as you tour it at your own leisure.

Nearby hotel:

- The Duomo is ideally close to a number of hotels, making access for guests simple. The cost of lodging will change depending on the type of hotel, the time of year, and the amenities.

Some popular options include.

San Michele hotel (+390575603673). And

Hotel Villa Marsili (+39 0575 629309).

It is advisable to contact each hotel directly to inquire about availability and current rates.

Nearby restaurants:

Enjoy the mouthwatering Tuscan cuisine at restaurants close to the Duomo. Among the notable choices are

Restaurant Dardano : (+39 0575 601944)
La Loggetta Restaurant :(+39 0575 630502).

The price of a meal will change based on the menu, the dishes ordered, and individual preferences. It is advised to contact the restaurants directly to inquire about bookings and current prices.

Awe-inspiring architectural splendor, priceless works of art, and spiritual significance of this historical landmark can all be appreciated by paying a visit to the Cortona Cathedral, or Duomo. Spend some time marveling at its beauty, taking in the calm environment, and seeing the centuries of history that have seeped into its holy halls.

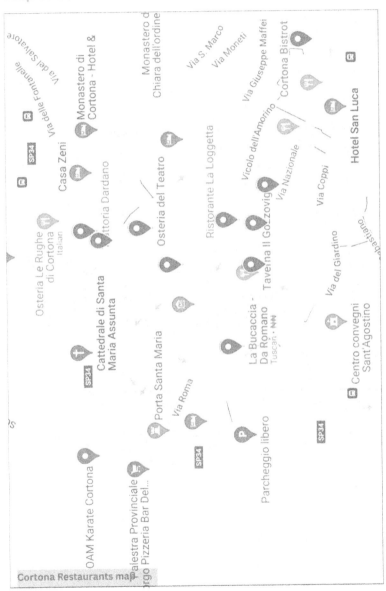

Cortona Restaurants map

Located just outside of Cortona, Eremo Le Celle is a mesmerizing attraction that provides a peaceful haven and a window into the area's spiritual history. Everything you need to know about this amazing website is provided below:

Address: Case Sparse, 73, 52044 Torreone, CortonaAR, Italy.

Phone: +390575601017

Website: www.lcelledicortona.it

Hours of Operation and Closing:

You can explore Eremo Le Celle's tranquil surroundings because it is normally open to visitors only during certain hours. For the most up-to-date information, it is advised to confirm the most recent opening and closing times with the neighborhood tourist information office or directly with Eremo Le Celle.

Distance from Cortona:

Eremo Le Celle is located about 7 kilometers (4.3 miles) from Cortona town. Depending on the route chosen and the kind of transportation employed, the amount of time needed to go between the two locations can change. The normal driving time from Eremo Le Celle to Cortona town is 15 minutes.

Closest Airport:

The closest international airport to Cortona is Perugia San Francesco d'Assisi Airport (PEG), which is situated around 55 kilometers (34 miles) from Eremo Le Celle. Typically, it takes an hour or so to drive from the airport to Eremo Le Celle, depending on traffic.

Regarding the closest train station, Terontola-Cortona Station, also known as Camucia-Cortona Station, is the one that is most convenient to Eremo Le Celle. It is situated in Camucia, a town that is roughly 9 kilometers (5.6 miles) away from Eremo Le Celle. By car or cab, it takes roughly 20 minutes to get to Eremo Le Celle from the train station.

It's crucial to remember that these distances and travel times are approximations and may vary depending on the route used and traffic conditions. Before arranging your trip, it is a good idea to check for any updates or alterations to the available modes of transportation and their schedules.

What to see:

You will be welcomed by a group of tiny stone cells, chapels, and a charming church when you arrive to Eremo Le Celle. Discover this hermitage's simplicity and beauty by exploring the tranquil surroundings. Admire the serene courtyards, the modest chapel interiors decorated with holy art, and the peaceful, contemplative surroundings that characterize the area.

What to do:

Eremo Le Celle provides a peaceful setting perfect for introspection, meditation, and private reflection. Enjoy the serenity of the surroundings by taking a leisurely stroll along the serene walks and letting yourself be carried away by the spiritual atmosphere. This is a great chance to escape the outer world and find comfort in the quiet surroundings of the hermitage.

How to tour:

You can take your time at Eremo Le Celle and take in all the peace and spiritual significance of the place by going at your own leisure.

There may also be guided tours that offer explanations of the hermitage's history, architecture, and religious importance. For further information, ask for guided tours at the destination or at the neighborhood tourist office.

Nearby hotel:

There aren't any hotels close to Eremo Le Celle because it's outside of Cortona. However, Cortona itself has a variety of lodging options that provide a range of amenities and comfort levels.

Several well-liked lodgings in Cortona include
Hotel San Michele (+39 0575 603673).
Villa Marsili Hotel (+39 0575 629309).

It is advised to contact the hotels directly to inquire about their most recent rates, availability, and any added services they provide.

Restaurant in the Area

After visiting Eremo Le Celle, return to Cortona to sate your appetite at one of the many eateries providing delectable Tuscan fare.

Trattoria Dardano: which may be reached at +39 0575 601944) and

La Loggetta Restaurant: (tel. +39 0575 630502).

The price of a meal will vary based on the foods ordered and individual preferences. For the most recent prices, reservations, and any special dietary needs, get in touch with the restaurants directly.

The tranquillity of the surroundings and the area's rich religious history can be experienced peacefully and spiritually during a trip to Eremo Le Celle. Spend some time exploring the hermitage, taking in the serene ambiance, and admiring the simplicity and beauty of this mesmerizing location.

Map of Le Celle Eremo

Le celle Eremo map

Diocesan museum

A must-see destination for fans of art and history is the Museo Diocesano, which is situated in the center of Cortona. Here is all you should know to maximize your time there:

Address: Piazza del Duomo, 1 , 52044 Cortona AR, Italy.
Phone: +390577286300
www.cortonatuseibellezza.it
Hours of Operation and Closing:

The museum is open during particular times, usually from early in the morning until late in the afternoon. It is advised to check the opening and closing hours with the museum directly or with the neighborhood tourist information office to make sure your visit will fit with the current schedule.

Distance from Cortona:

Museo Diocesano is inside the town of Cortona, so the distance between it and the town is not very great. As a result, the distance can be regarded as insignificant.

Closest Airport:

The closest international airport to Cortona is Perugia San Francesco d'Assisi Airport (PEG), which is positioned around 60 kilometers (37 miles) from Cortona. Depending on traffic, it normally takes an hour or so to drive from the airport to Cortona.

Closest Train Station:

The Terontola-Cortona Station, also known as Camucia-Cortona Station, is the one that is most convenient to Cortona. It is situated in Camucia, a village that is about 4 kilometers (2.5 miles) from Cortona. Cortona may be reached from the train station in about 10 minutes by vehicle or taxi.

What to see:

Get lost in the historical and aesthetic riches kept in Museo Diocesano. Paintings, sculptures, manuscripts, and other religious artifacts are among the museum's outstanding collection. Admire the works of art produced by renowned artists that represent a variety of artistic eras and styles and provide a window into the rich cultural legacy of the area.

What to do:

Spend some time admiring each piece of art's amazing craftsmanship and historical relevance. Read the educational descriptions, interact with the exhibits, and allow yourself to be enthralled by the tales they reveal. Your chance to gain a deeper understanding of religious art and its significance in the community is exceptional thanks to the museum.

Tour tips:

Here are some suggestions to improve your time at Museo Diocesano:

- If a guided tour is offered, take advantage of it to learn more about the artwork and its historical setting.
- Use any audio guides or educational resources the museum may have supplied to conduct a self-guided tour.

- Plan your visit for a less busy time to properly enjoy the exhibits in a calmer setting.
- Bring a journal or a sketchbook so you can record your thoughts and ideas as well as produce original artwork that is inspired by the museum's collection.

Insight:

A unique view into Cortona's cultural and artistic legacy is provided by Museo Diocesano. It demonstrates the enormous impact that religion has had on local art and invites visitors to investigate the spiritual and cultural importance of each work.

Hotels close by:

Although there aren't any hotels very next to the Museo Diocesano, there are a lot of choices nearby in Cortona.

Two suggestions are provided below:

San Michele Hotel

This quaint hotel is situated at Via Guelfa 15, and it has cozy rooms with features like free Wi-Fi, a restaurant, and a bar. Call +39 0575 603673 for reservations and questions.

Villa Marsili Hotel

This exquisite hotel is located in Via delle Iannaccone, 48, and offers tastefully furnished rooms, a garden, and a terrace with panoramic views. There is a bar, free Wi-Fi, and a complimentary breakfast available for guests. Call +39 0575 629309 for reservations and information.

The price of lodging may change based on the time of year, the type of room, and the availability. It is advised to speak with the hotels directly to learn about their current pricing and any added services they provide.

Restaurant in the Area

Enjoy the flavors of Tuscan cuisine at one of Cortona's charming restaurants after seeing the Museo Diocesano. Think about these choices:

Restaurant Dardano:

This quaint trattoria is situated at Via Dardano 24 and serves typical Tuscan cuisine. Call +39 0575 601944 for reservations or questions.

Loggetta:

This restaurant, which is located at Via Nazionale 33, offers a classy dining experience with a menu that highlights regional delicacies. Call +39 0575 630502 to reserve a table or for additional details.

The price of a meal at these establishments can change based on the foods ordered and individual preferences. It is best to get in touch with the eateries directly to inquire about the most recent menu items, make reservations, and discuss any dietary restrictions you may have.

Visitors are encouraged to experience Cortona's rich cultural past by visiting the Museo Diocesano, which houses an extensive collection of religious art and historical items. Everyone who enters this top destination is guaranteed an enriching and memorable experience, from the enthralling exhibitions to the adjacent hotels and eateries.

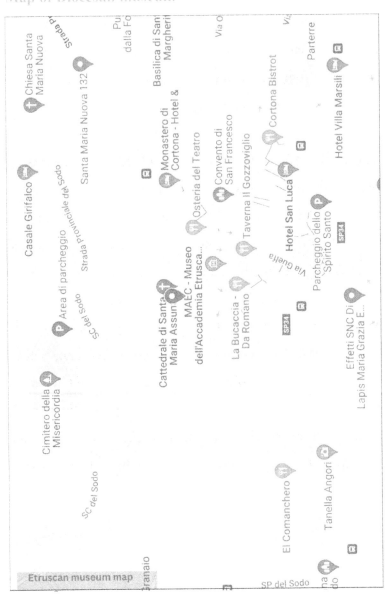

Etruscan museum map

Academia Etrusca

One of the most popular attractions in Cortona is the Accademia Etrusca, a renowned cultural institution. Here is a thorough guide to help you get the most out of your trip:

Address: Piazza Luca Signorelli 9, 52044 Cortona AR, Italy.

Phone: +390575630415

Website: www.cortonamec.org

Hours of Operation and Closing:

Visitors are welcome at the Accademia Etrusca during specific times each day. Check the academy's most recent opening and closing times or ask at the neighborhood tourist information center to make sure you don't miss out.

Distance from Cortona:

The distance between the Accademia Etrusca and Cortona town might be regarded insignificant because the Accademia Etrusca is situated within Cortona town itself.

Closeset Airport

The closest international airport to Cortona is Perugia San Francesco d'Assisi Airport (PEG), which is positioned around 60 kilometers (37 miles) from Cortona. Depending on traffic, it normally takes an hour or so to drive from the airport to Cortona.

Closest Train Station

The Terontola-Cortona Station, also known as Camucia-Cortona Station, is the one that is most convenient to Cortona. It is situated in Camucia, a village that is about 4 kilometers (2.5 miles) from Cortona. Cortona may be reached from the train station in about 10 minutes by vehicle or taxi.

Please be aware that these travel distances and times are only estimates that may change according to the precise route used and the current traffic conditions. Before arranging your trip, it is a good idea to check for any updates or alterations to the available modes of transportation and their schedules.

What to see:

Get ready to be engulfed by the abundance of historical relics and artistic treasures that adorn the Accademia Etrusca. The academy is home to a varied collection of Roman and Etruscan artifacts as well as magnificent Renaissance works of art. Learn about the rich cultural history of the area by exploring antique ceramics, sculptures, and manuscripts.

What to do:

Enjoy each exhibit's excellent craftsmanship and historical relevance at your own pace. Interact with the objects, examine their enlightening descriptions, and learn the intriguing tales that surround them. Both history buffs and art connoisseurs will find the Accademia Etrusca to be an engaging experience because it offers a captivating trip through history and art.

Tour tips:

Follow these advice to get the most of your trip to Accademia Etrusca:

- To obtain a deeper understanding of the exhibits and historical background, think about taking a guided tour.
- Utilize any audio tours or informational resources offered at the academy to conduct a self-guided tour.
- If it's permitted, take pictures of your favorite items to preserve them as souvenirs of your trip.
- Be aware and respectful of the displayed items because there can be prohibitions on touching the relics in some places.

Insight:

The Accademia Etrusca is a bustling cultural center that supports study and the arts in addition to being a storehouse for priceless artifacts from antiquity. It was founded in the 18th century and has been essential in protecting and promoting Cortona's rich legacy.

Hotels close by:

While there aren't any hotels just next to Accademia Etrusca, there are plenty of comfortable places to stay close by. Two suggestions are provided below:

San Michele Hotel

This quaint hotel is situated at Via Guelfa 15, and it has cozy rooms with features like free Wi-Fi, a restaurant, and a bar. Call +39 0575 603673 for reservations and questions.

Villa Marsili Hotel

This exquisite hotel is located in Via delle Iannaccone, 48, and offers tasteful lly furnished rooms, a garden, and a terrace with panoramic views. There is a bar, free Wi-Fi, and a complimentary breakfast available for guests. Call +39 0575 629309 for reservations and information.

The price of lodging may change based on the time of year, the type of room, and the availability. It is advised to speak with the hotels directly to learn about their current pricing and any added services they provide.

Restaurant in the Area

After visiting Accademia Etrusca, treat yourself to some delectable Tuscan fare at one of the surrounding eateries. Here are a few possibilities:

Restaurant Dardano:

This quaint trattoria is situated at Via Dardano 24 and serves typical Tuscan cuisine. Call +39 0575 601944 for reservations or questions.

The La Loggetta Restaurant

Ristorante La Loggetta, which is located at Via Nazionale 33, provides a posh dining experience with a menu that highlights regional delicacies. Call +39 0575 630502 to secure a table or for more information.

The price of a meal at these establishments can change based on the foods ordered and individual preferences. It is best to get in touch with the eateries directly to inquire about the most recent menu items, make reservations, and discuss any dietary restrictions you may have.

With its impressive collection of artifacts and antiques, Accademia Etrusca enables guests to take an enthralling trip through history. Visitors who value history, art, and the local culture will have an enriching and unforgettable time at this top attraction in Cortona, from the breathtaking displays to the close-by hotels and eateries.

Villa Bramasole

One of Cortona's greatest attractions, Villa Bramasole provides an enthralling look at Tuscany's natural splendor. You should be aware of the following before going:

Address: Localita Torreone, 151, 52044 Cortona AR, Italy.

Website: www.cortonamia.com

Hours of Operation and Closing:

Depending on the season and special occasions, Villa Bramasole's opening and closing times may change. To guarantee entry to the villa's interior, it is advised to enquire in advance about the visiting hours or sign up for a guided tour.

Distance from Cortona:

The villa known as Villa Bramasole, which was featured in the novel and film "Under the Tuscan Sun," is situated outside of Cortona. Depending on the villa's unique position, the distance from Villa Bramasole to Cortona town will vary. However, because Cortona is a small town, it is usually within a few kilometers or less.

Closest airport

The closest international airport to Cortona is Perugia San Francesco d'Assisi Airport (PEG), which is positioned around 60 kilometers (37 miles) from Cortona. Depending on traffic, it normally takes an hour or so to drive from the airport to Cortona.

Closest Train Station

The Terontola-Cortona Station, also known as Camucia-Cortona Station, is the one that is most convenient to Cortona. It is situated in Camucia, a village that is about 4 kilometers (2.5 miles) from Cortona. Cortona may be reached from the train station in about 10 minutes by vehicle or taxi.

What to see:

Beautiful historical Villa Bramasole displays traditional Tuscan architecture and scenery. A pleasure to behold are the villa's lovely gardens and the expansive views of the surrounding countryside.

What to do:

Visitors can still enjoy Villa Bramasole's splendor from the outside even though it is a privately held property and not accessible to the general public. Wander casually around the villa's exterior to take in its stunning gardens and architecture. Additionally, the picturesque location offers a fantastic chance for photography.

Tour guide:

It is important to respect the privacy of the home and its owners because Villa Bramasole is not accessible to the general public for tours. Even if you are unable to visit the villa itself, you can still have a great day by exploring the surrounding regions and taking pictures from a distance.

Insight:

Villa Bramasole is a sought-after destination for tourists looking to experience the true spirit of Tuscany due to its charm and attractiveness, which made it famous as the setting for Frances Mayes' well-known memoir "Under the Tuscan Sun."

Hotels close by:

While there aren't any hotels very next to Villa Bramasole, Cortona offers a variety of places to stay. Two suggestions are provided below:

San Michele Hotel

This quaint hotel is situated at Via Guelfa 15, and it has cozy rooms with features like free Wi-Fi, a restaurant, and a bar. Call +39 0575 603673 for reservations and questions.

Villa Marsili Hotel

This exquisite hotel is located in Via delle Iannaccone, 48, and offers tastefully furnished rooms, a garden, and a terrace with panoramic views. There is a bar, free Wi-Fi, and a complimentary breakfast available for guests. Call +39 0575 629309 for reservations and information.

The price of lodging may change based on the time of year, the type of room, and the availability. It is advised to speak with the hotels directly to learn about their current pricing and any added services they provide.

Restaurant in the Area

Due to the fact that Villa Bramasole is a private residence, it lacks a restaurant and other public dining options. However, Cortona, a nearby town, has a broad selection of great eateries providing genuine Tuscan fare. Explore the neighborhood restaurants in Cortona and savor the mouthwatering cuisine of the area for the best eating options.

Map of Villa Bramasole

San Domenico Basilica

One of Cortona's main tourist destinations, San Domenico Basilica offers a rich historical and architectural experience. You should be aware of the following before going:

Address: Piazza San Domenico, 1, 52044 Cortona, Italy.

Hours of Operation and Closing:

The San Domenico Basilica typically welcomes tourists during the day. However, it is wise to double-check the precise opening and closing times as they may change based on the time of year and religious occasions.

Distance from Cortona:

In the center of Cortona sits the stunning church known as San Domenico Basilica. Due to the basilica's location inside the town of Cortona, there is not much of a gap between the two.

Closest Airport

The closest international airport to Cortona is Perugia San Francesco d'Assisi Airport (PEG), which is positioned about 60 kilometers (37 miles) away. Depending on traffic, it normally takes an hour or so to drive from the airport to Cortona.

The Terontola-Cortona Station, also known as Camucia-Cortona Station, is the one that is most convenient to Cortona. It is situated in Camucia, a village that is about 3 kilometers (1.8 miles) from Cortona. Cortona may be reached from the train station in 5 minutes or less by vehicle or taxi.

Closest train station

Since San Domenico Basilica is in the center of Cortona, visitors may easily walk around the town and travel by car or public transportation to get to the airport and train station.

What to see:

The basilica is renowned for its breathtaking Gothic design and exquisite frescoes, which include the well-known Annunciation by Fra Angelico. Admire the interior's delicate decorations, which are embellished with religious items and pieces of art that highlight Cortona's rich cultural legacy.

What to do:

Take your time when seeing San Domenico Basilica to appreciate the splendor of the structure and become fully aware of its historical significance. Take a moment for calm study and contemplation while admiring the artistic craftsmanship of the sculptures and frescoes.

Tour guide:

Here are some suggestions to make your visit to San Domenico Basilica more enjoyable:

- When attending places of worship, dress appropriately, covering your shoulders and knees as a symbol of respect.
- To learn more about the basilica's past and significance, think about taking a guided tour or getting an audio guide.

- The frescoes and artwork should be carefully examined because they frequently contain hidden meanings and stories.

- To respect the solemn ambiance of the basilica, turn off your phone and act quietly.

Insight:

The San Domenico Basilica is a symbol of Cortona's cultural and artistic legacy. Visitors come from all over the world to see its stunning architecture and priceless artworks, which offer a window into the area's diverse cultural heritage.

Hotels close by:

San Domenico Basilica is not far from a number of hotels. Two suggestions are provided below:

The San Luca Hotel

This conveniently located hotel near Piazza Garibaldi, 1 offers cozy accommodations, complimentary WiFi, and a bar. Contact +39 0575 605267 for reservations and questions.

Italy Hotel:

This lovely hotel, which is situated at Piazza Italia 5, has a restaurant, a rooftop patio, and well-appointed rooms. Free Wi-Fi, a bar, and a complementary breakfast are just a few of the amenities available to guests. Call +39 0575 603450 for reservations and information.

The price of lodging may change based on the time of year, the type of room, and the availability. It is advised to speak with the hotels directly to learn about their current pricing and any added services they provide.

Restaurant in the Area

There are many top-notch restaurants in Cortona that serve delicious Tuscan fare. San Domenico Basilica doesn't have a dedicated restaurant, but you can explore the restaurants in the area for a pleasant eating experience. It is preferable to speak with nearby businesses or consult internet sites that offer the most recent details on Cortona's dining alternatives for restaurant recommendations and queries.

CHAPTER 4

Cortona has a wide range of thrilling outdoor pursuits that will enthrall your senses and leave you with priceless memories.Be careful to check the local calendar for festivals and outdoor events. Throughout the year, Cortona hosts a number of events, such as wine tastings, food fairs, and music festivals. These gatherings offer a wonderful chance to interact with locals and other tourists while also being immersed in the local culture.

Therefore, Cortona has something to offer everyone, whether you're an enthusiastic hiker, cyclist, rock climber, or just someone who enjoys the beauty of nature. Get ready to explore the allure of this quaint Tuscan hamlet and engage on spectacular outdoor excursions.

Trekking

Outdoor enthusiasts will find plenty of things to do in Cortona that will allow them to fully appreciate the spectacular splendor of the area's landscapes. Hiking stands out among the many outdoor activities as a stimulating and satisfying activity that enables you to explore the area's natural treasures.

Cortona is home to a network of well-kept hiking paths that meander through picturesque vineyards, lush woodlands, and rolling hills. These paths are suitable for hikers of all skill levels, offering everything from easy strolls to strenuous treks that put your stamina to the test and pay off with stunning views.

The Sentiero della Bonifica, a charming path that follows the path of an old canal, is one of Cortona's most popular hiking trails. You'll be treated to magnificent views of the surrounding countryside as you stroll along this trail, which is filled with olive trees, vineyards, and ancient farmhouses. All skill levels can enjoy this easy trip, which offers a wonderful opportunity to see the rural charm of the area.

Consider climbing Monte Sant'Egidio, the tallest peak in the Cortona region, for a more difficult journey. This trail rewards your efforts with panoramic vistas of the Tuscan countryside as it leads you through lush forests and mountainous terrain. A sense of success and a well-earned relaxation are offered by the summit's stunning view, which extends as far as the eye can see.

A lovely valley with a variety of sceneries, the Val di Chiana is a well-known trekking location close to Cortona. This region is a nature lover's paradise with its gentle hills, green meadows, attractive villages, and serene lakes. The numerous options to explore Val di Chiana's grandeur on foot are unlimited, giving visitors a complete sense of the area's natural splendor.

It's crucial to be prepared before setting out on a trekking expedition in Cortona. Carry a backpack with water, snacks, and a trail guide. Wear strong, comfortable shoes. Additionally, it's a good idea to check the weather and select a path based on your degree of fitness and interests.

Spend some time admiring the beauty all around you as you trek through the lovely countryside. Allow yourself to be totally present in the moment while taking a deep breath of fresh air and listening to the sounds of nature. You can come across indigenous flora and fauna, quaint towns, and undiscovered treasures along the journey, making each step an exploration of Cortona's own appeal.

In addition to being a form of exercise, hiking in Cortona is a journey that renews your spirit, fosters a deep sense of peace, and helps you connect with nature. Hiking in Cortona will likely leave you with priceless memories and a deep appreciation for the area's natural wonders, whether you select an easy trail for a leisurely stroll or a strenuous route for a more adventurous experience.

Cortona hiking is an exceptional outdoor sport that enables you to interact with the area's natural splendor and fully experience its varied landscapes. Cortona provides a variety of hiking alternatives that are ideal for all ability levels, from easy trails to demanding summits. So lace up your hiking boots, go on an expedition, and watch Cortona's mesmerizing beauty develop.

Walking Routes

Walking trails stand out among these outdoor activities as a delightful opportunity to explore the alluring surroundings that surround this quaint town. Cortona is home to a system of lovely walking paths that meander over undulating hills, historic olive groves, and exquisite vineyards. These routes offer chances for leisurely strolls, energizing treks, and everything in between, catering to walkers of all abilities.

The Sentiero del Monte S. Egidio, which takes you to the top of Monte Sant'Egidio, is one of Cortona's most popular walking routes. You will be rewarded with expansive views of the Tuscan countryside and the town of Cortona as you climb this picturesque path. Both casual walkers and experienced hikers can use the well-marked track, which has varied degrees of difficulty.

The Strada delle Vigne, or "Wine Road," is another lovely walking route in Cortona that passes past magnificent vineyards and lets you take in the splendor of the Tuscan wine-growing region. You'll have the chance to learn about the area's winemaking customs and possibly even try some local wines at vineyard tasting facilities as you wander along this picturesque road.

The Sentiero del Bosco walk offers a lovely trek through lush forests and peaceful meadows for those looking for a more intense encounter with nature. As you stroll down this tranquil walk, you can re-establish your connection with nature as you take in the vivid hues of the wildflowers, the gently air, and the sounds of singing birds. It provides a tranquil and restorative experience as the ideal get-away from the everyday craziness.

It's crucial to be ready when exploring Cortona's walking routes. Dress in layers, bring a small bag with water, food, and a trail map, and wear comfortable walking shoes. To ensure that Cortona's natural beauty is preserved for future generations to enjoy, always follow trail etiquette, respect nature, and leave no trace.

Spend some time getting lost in the surroundings as you stroll through Cortona's walking trails. Engage all of your senses as you take in the enticing smells of the countryside, listen to nature's calming noises, and gaze in awe at the breathtaking landscapes that appear before you. You might come across endearing fauna, adorable farmhouses, or even chance upon undiscovered treasures that capture Cortona's authentic rustic appeal.

A transforming experience that enables you to connect with nature, find peace, and develop a greater appreciation for the area's natural treasures, hiking Cortona's paths is more than just a physical activity. Cortona's walking routes offer a riveting adventure that will leave you with treasured memories and a renewed feeling of wonder, whether you opt for a leisurely stroll or a more strenuous hike.

The walking trails in Cortona serve as a doorway to the area's natural beauty, enabling tourists to set out on an unforgettable journey through its captivating landscapes. These pathways provide walkers of all abilities with a variety of experiences, from expansive vistas to tranquil vineyards. So put on your walking shoes, follow your curiosity, and see Cortona's mesmerizing beauty emerge before your eyes.

Vineyard tours and wine tasting

A lovely outdoor activity that enables you to immerse yourself in the rich winemaking heritage and taste the exquisite flavors of the area is participating in wine tasting and vineyard tours.

Beyond Cortona, there are several vineyards and wineries that display the creativity and ardor of Tuscan winemakers. These opportunities offer a chance to explore the world of viticulture, learn about winemaking processes, and savor excellent wines that perfectly capture Tuscany.

The region's undulating hills and rich soils are ideal for growing a range of grape varietals, producing wines that are well regarded all over the world. You will have the opportunity to taste both well-known Tuscan classics like

Chianti, Brunello di Montalcino, and Vino Nobile di Montepulciano as well as lesser-known regional treasures as you set off on a wine tasting adventure.

Many wineries in the vicinity of Cortona provide guided tours that let you see their magnificent estates and vineyards. You will be escorted through the winemaking process by knowledgeable guides who will share insights on grape growth, harvest, and the nuances of fermentation and aging. You'll develop a greater understanding of the skill and commitment that go into making remarkable wines.

Take the time to enjoy the gorgeous surroundings as you stroll through the vineyards. Vineyards are frequently tucked away among undulating hills covered in rows of lush grapevines, giving rise to a magnificent setting that captures the essence of the Tuscan countryside. As you inhale the earthy aromas of the vineyards and take in the brilliant hues of the scenery, capture the beauty with your senses.

In this location, there are more options for wine tasting than just sipping it in a basement. You can enjoy your wine amidst vineyards or on picturesque terraces thanks to the several wineries that provide samples in lovely outdoor settings. You can more thoroughly appreciate the tastes, scents, and nuances of each sip thanks to the peaceful environment, which also enriches the sensory experience.

Consider taking a guided tour or hiring a local expert who can create a custom schedule based on your tastes to get the most out of your wine tasting and vineyard excursions. They may lead you to undiscovered jewels, suggest the top wineries to visit, and offer insightful information about the area's wine culture.

Don't be shy about talking to winemakers and vineyard owners as you learn more about the wine industry in the Cortona area. They frequently have a deep love for what they do and are willing to impart their wisdom. Ask them questions, pay close attention to their answers, and allow their enthusiasm to spark your own admiration for the craft of winemaking.

It's crucial to plan your mobility appropriately when taking part in wine tasting and vineyard excursions and to consume alcohol sensibly. To ensure you can thoroughly enjoy the wines without worrying about the trip back, think about hiring a driver or joining organized trips that provide transportation.

You may immerse yourself in the complex world of Tuscan wines by participating in wine tastings and vineyard visits close to Cortona. You can taste the history, fervor, and skill that go into making these extraordinary wines with every sip. So raise your glass, take in the vines' splendor, and allow the tastes of Tuscany to dance on your tongue.

Beach excursion

Not too far away, you may set out on a pleasant beach excursion and unwind by the coast. For a soothing outdoor pastime, explore the local beaches and take in the beautiful combination of sun, sand, and crystal-clear waters. You can reach the lovely beaches along the Tuscan coast in a short drive from Cortona. There are options to suit every desire, whether you're looking for an energetic environment or a quiet place to unwind.

You may explore a variety of sceneries on the region's beaches, which have a combination of sandy stretches, pebbly shoreline, and rocky coves. Enjoy the quiet atmosphere while relaxing with your feet in the warm sand while you soak up the Mediterranean sun, or choose a spot in the shade under an umbrella.

You are invited to have a refreshing swim or participate in a variety of water sports in the crystal-clear turquoise seas. Discover the thriving marine life below the surface as you swim, snorkel, or paddle around the shoreline. You can even try your hand at water activities like kayaking, windsurfing, or stand-up paddleboarding if you're looking for a little more adventure.

You can experience coastal Italian life as you visit the local beaches and quaint seaside towns and villages. Enjoy gelato, stroll the promenades, and dine at neighborhood restaurants that serve delectable seafood meals. Accept the relaxed mood and savor the coastal charm that the area has to offer.

Castiglione della Pescaia, which is around 100 kilometers from Cortona's main town, Marina di Grosseto, which is about 110 kilometers away, and Punta, Ala, which is about 135 kilometers, are some of the well-known beaches nearby. Every beach has a distinctive personality and amenities that range from beach clubs with umbrellas and sunbeds to more secluded sections of shoreline. To explore the variety and discover your favorite beach, think about visiting many.

Pack the necessary beach items, including sunscreen, hats, towels, and swimwear, to make the most of your beach vacation. Remember to pack a picnic or pick up some regional treats to enjoy a coastal feast.

Additionally, there are scheduled beach tours available if you prefer a hassle-free experience. These trips include transportation, allowing you to unwind and enjoy the voyage without the burden of navigating and parking.

It's crucial to consider local laws and the weather while organizing your beach trip, especially during the busiest summer months. Planning ahead and making your reservations is a good idea because certain beaches may have parking limitations or demand reservations for beach clubs.

For anyone looking for some sun, relaxation, and a taste of the Italian coastline, taking a beach trip near Cortona is a fantastic outdoor activity. The adjacent beaches offer a chance to relax, rest, and savor Tuscany's coastal beauty, whether you choose crowded beach towns or undiscovered jewels off the beaten route. So gather your beach supplies, take a deep breath of the briny air, and let the calming sounds of the waves wash your concerns away.

Food tours and cooking classes

Cooking workshops and food excursions are popular outdoor pursuits in Cortona where you can fully immerse yourself in the gastronomic delights of Tuscany. Learn the secrets of Tuscan cooking and how to make classic dishes with local, fresh ingredients. Engage in conversation with experienced chefs who will lead you through the culinary process, from choosing ingredients at the neighborhood markets to creating and enjoying your own creations.

Cooking workshops offer practical learning opportunities where you may pick up useful cooking skills and recipes that have been passed down through the years. As you chop, mix, and season your way to making delectable Tuscan foods, interact in a fun setting. These lessons provide a thorough exploration of the region's culinary traditions, from freshly cooked pasta and sauces to decadent sweets.

You can explore the thriving local food scene and sample a variety of Tuscan specialties on food tours in Cortona. Join a guided tour to enjoy local specialties including pecorino cheese, cured meats, bruschetta, and fine wines at renowned trattorias, bakeries, and markets. Discover the origins and customs of each dish as skilled guides impart their knowledge.

Both cooking lessons and food excursions provide one-of-a-kind chances to interact with the local community and become familiar with Tuscan cuisine. These activities offer a fascinating and immersive experience that enables you to bring a piece of Cortona's culinary tradition home, regardless of whether you are an experienced cook or a food enthusiast.

CHAPTER 5

Y ou can choose from a variety of lodging options in Cortona to suit your interests and financial situation. The town provides travelers with a wide range of lodging options, from adorable boutique hotels to welcoming bed & breakfasts.

There are expensive hotels that offer magnificent accommodations, spa amenities, and breathtaking views of the surrounding countryside for visitors looking for a lavish and indulgent experience. These places frequently have on-site restaurants serving top-notch regional food, making for a really immersive experience.

Bed and breakfasts are a common accommodation option in Cortona if you want a more private and customized stay. These lodgings have comfortable rooms with distinctive decor, and many are run by kind hosts who are ready to impart their local expertise. When you stay at a bed and breakfast, you can get to know the locals and experience a cozy, homey atmosphere.

There are also holiday homes and apartments available in Cortona for those on a tight budget or those looking for a self-catering option. These offer the comfort of a fully functional kitchen and the flexibility to set your own timetable. They are especially well suited for families or groups who seek a more autonomous and adaptable lodging alternative.

Whatever kind of lodging you pick, Cortona will provide you with convenience, friendliness, and a dash of genuine Italian charm. The town is the ideal site for a delightful visit in the heart of Tuscany due to its setting amidst rolling hills and its rich historical and cultural history.

Hotel

Hotels in Cortona provide a variety of extras to make your stay more enjoyable. You can anticipate tastefully decorated rooms with cozy furnishings, cutting-edge amenities, and thoughtful extras that enhance your comfort. Some hotels have their own restaurants where you may enjoy delectable Tuscan food made with fresh local ingredients.

The town's attractive setting offers a tranquil getaway that is bordered by lovely scenery and vineyards. Whether you're traveling for work or pleasure, Cortona hotels provide a tranquil environment where you may unwind.

Hotel San Michele

The historic center of Cortona is where you'll find the Hotel San Michele. A Renaissance mansion that was restored gave birth to this national monument, which is also home to a Masaccio school fresco from the 15th century. The hotel, which has been tastefully restored, offers classic, superior, junior, and suite accommodations, some of which have a private balcony with a view and are furnished with modern conveniences.

A covered garage, a separate bathroom, and air conditioning. On request, massages, cooking lessons, and excursions are offered. On request: "La Torretta," a relaxation space with a hot tub and a 360-degree view.

The essential information is as follows:

Cost price:

- The price to stay at Hotel San Michele varies according to the season and room type. For the most precise and recent pricing information, it is advised to check their website or get in touch with them directly.

Address: Via 15, 52044, Cortona, Italy

Phone: +39 0575 603140

Website:

- You may visit Hotel San Michele's official website to find out more about the hotel, including information about available rooms, facilities, and extra services.

www.hotel san michele cortona.com

Room types:

Bridal suite

Non-smoking rooms

Suites

Family rooms

Room features:

Air conditioning

Housekeeping

Room service

Safe

Telephone

VIP room facilities

Minibar

Flatscreen TV

Amenities

Paid private parking on-site

Free High Speed Internet (WiFi)

Hot tub

Free breakfast

Hiking

Banquet room

Manicure

Baggage storage

The rooms of Hotel San Michele are cozy and elegantly furnished with the goal of giving visitors a comfortable and enjoyable stay. It is a great option for travelers to Cortona because to its handy location, welcoming staff, and useful services. Hotel San Michele provides a cozy base for your time in Cortona, whether you plan to visit the town's historical attractions, eat some regional food, or just relax and take in the scenery.

Cortona Resort & Spa

Travelers visiting Cortona should consider staying at the Cortona Resort & Spa, which provides a welcoming environment for families as well as a number of convenient amenities to make your stay more enjoyable. The Cortona Resort & Spa's rooms come equipped with a flat-screen TV, a minibar, air conditioning, and complimentary internet so that visitors can stay connected.

Additionally, visitors can take advantage of room service and a concierge when staying at Cortona Resort & Spa. Additionally, a pool and free breakfast are available. Do you require parking? The resort and spa at Cortona offer free parking.

Considering that well-known attractions like Santa Maria del Calcinaio and Belvedere di Cortona are conveniently close by, visitors of Cortona Resort & Spa can simply visit some of Cortona's most well-known attractions.

Cortona Resort & Spa is ideally placed close to Osteria del Teatro, La Bucaccia da Romano, and La Loggetta - La Locanda nel Loggiato if you enjoy Italian cuisine.

Seeking to discover some landmark? Then go no further than the popular Cortona attractions Bramasole (1.0 mi), MAEC - Museo dell'Accademia Etrusca (1.2 mi), and Piazza della Repubblica (1.1 mi), all of which are conveniently close to the hotel.

These are the key facts you need to be aware of:

Cost:

- Depending on the type of room booked, the time of year, and any available discounts, the cost of a stay at Cortona Resort & Spa may change.

Address:

- The hotel is located at Nucleo Campaccio 5/8, 52044 Cortona, Italy, tucked away in the lovely Tuscan countryside.

Phone:

- all Cortona Resort & Spa at +39 0575 601433 for more information, to check on availability, or to book a reservation.

Website:

- Visit Cortona Resort & Spa's official website at to learn more about the amenities, features, and services it provides.

www.cortonaresortandspa.com

Room types:

Non-smoking rooms

Suites

Family rooms

Room features

Bathrobes

Air conditioning

Room service

Safe

Telephone

Minibar

Flatscreen TV

Complimentary toiletries

Property amenities:

Free parking

Free High Speed Internet (WiFi)

Pool

Fitness / spa locker rooms

Free breakfast

Walking tours

Pets Allowed (Dog / Pet Banquet room
Friendly)

Visitors can enjoy an opulent and revitalizing experience at Cortona Resort & Spa. It offers the ideal balance of relaxation and indulgence with its beautiful accommodations, cutting-edge spa amenities, and stunning views of the surrounding terrain. Visitors looking for a peaceful hideaway in the heart of Tuscany are guaranteed a great stay thanks to the resort's dedicated personnel and first-rate amenities.

The San Luca Hotel

It takes 15 minutes to get from Hotel San Luca in Cortona's old center to Lake Trasimeno. It offers elegant, air-conditioned rooms with a minibar and satellite TV.On the hotel's patio, you can see the entire surrounding landscape in its entirety. On the covered terrace, there is a gym, and there is a separate sun terrace with a hot tub.The entire building offers free WiFi. The front desk is available round-the-clock.The A1 highway is 25 minutes' drive from the hotel and is located approximately 3 km from Camucia di Cortona Station. Perugia may be reached in 40 minutes by vehicle.

Address:

Piazza Giuseppe Garibaldi 2, 52044, Cortona Italy

Room types

Bridal suite	Property amenities
Non-smoking rooms	Free public parking nearby
Family rooms	
	Free High Speed Internet (WiFi)
Room features	Free breakfast
Soundproof rooms	Hiking
Air conditioning	Pets Allowed (Dog / Pet Friendly)
Desk	
Housekeeping	Car hire
Private balcony	Banquet room
Refrigerator	Meeting rooms
Flatscreen TV	
Complimentary toiletrie	

Cortona Resort - Le Terre dei Cavalieri

The estate is made up of a Farmhouse and a Leopoldina that were constructed in the 18th century during the Grand Dukes of Tuscany's vast reclamation of the Valdichiana. They once belonged to the Order of the Knights of Malta and St. Stephen. The historic Grand Ducal Farm of Creti and S. Caterina was guarded by the Order.

The restoration of these structures required several years of work, during which the old "cocciopesto" plaster was reestablished, walls were painted using natural stuccoed pigments while maintaining the fireplaces' original structure, vaults from the old stable were left empty and strengthened, and stucco was applied to the columns that define the surrounding landscape.

Today, they are able to provide you with this one-of-a-kind setting where you may have an intensive and singular experience, giving you the impression that you are a part of a setting where things have not changed and where the past seems to come to life every day in all of its charm and character. You can eat in a kitchen that once seated more than thirty people at once, sleep in a room made from an old cattle shed where farmers used to spend sleepless nights watching over their cows as they delivered their calves, sleep in a room with a "tracantone" bed, or sleep in a room made from an old dove tower, where farmers raised doves.

Fireplaces will tell you and bring back memories of tales shared when huddling around them on chilly winter nights.Paintings and photographs that illustrate ancient customs and ways of life are used to decorate the walls. The windows that open onto spectacular natural surroundings, such as the black mountains that tower over Cortona, the smooth and pleasant countryside, and the noble profile of Cortona, will provide you with the nicest views you will be able to see.

A singular observation, genuine peasant landscapes and tastes, a calming and unwinding impact, and a plethora of details expressing the sense of location.I'm looking forward to seeing you there to learn a lot more things that are beyond words

Address:

Loc. Fratta Santa Caterina 46, 52044, Cortona Italy

Room types

Non-smoking rooms

Suites

Family rooms

Room features

Air conditioning

Desk

Housekeeping

Safe

Refrigerator

Flatscreen TV

Bath / shower

Complimentary toiletries

Telephone

Hair dryer

Property amenities

Free parking

Free High Speed Internet (WiFi)

Pool

Restaurant

Babysitting

Children's television networks

Meeting rooms

Solarium

Wifi

Pool / beach towels

Infinity pool

Pool with view

Outdoor pool

Shallow end in pool

Breakfast available

Breakfast buffet

Snack bar

Special diet menus

BBQ facilities

Baggage storage

BBQ facilities

Baggage storage

Mosquito net

Non-smoking hotel

Outdoor furniture	Dry cleaning
Shared lounge / TV area	Laundry service
Sun loungers / beach chairs	Ironing service
Sun terrace	

Borgo il Melone

A place where the beauty of the surroundings is complemented by the leisurely pace of time. At Borgo il Melone, every holiday whim is realized just a short distance from the magnificent art cities of Cortona and Arezzo, next to Lake Trasimeno, on the border with Umbria.

Imagine yourself in a quaint 19th-century village amidst the verdant Tuscan hills, complete with elegant settings, sizable rooms and suites decorated in the traditional Tuscan manner, and a private garden with a swimming pool.

For those looking for tranquility in an upscale setting and private areas, surrounded by the unmatched beauty of a little 19th-century village close to the magnificent Tuscan art treasures of Cortona and Arezzo.

The perfect place for anyone looking to have meetings or professional gatherings in a luxurious and exclusive environment in a charming village. There is a meeting room that is furnished as well as numerous specialized services. An intimate and romantic environment to celebrate your wedding in opulent settings that will make the occasion magical and unforgettable.

Dimensions and capacity

Borgo Il Melone offers a variety of spaces for your most special day, including the Limonaia, where the wedding banquet finds its natural setting, a small private chapel for religious ceremonies, a magnificent garden (4 hectares), terraces with the most stirring views, and the fabulous swimming pool.

Built in 1864, The Limonaia is the ideal location to crown a wonderful wedding lunch. 190 square meters of space with a high ceiling, no columns, huge windows with pointed arches and colored mosaics that screen the sun's rays, and a magnificent dance of light. The garden of the Limonaia, which opens onto the long side of the building and provides countless options for the wedding banquet, could not be missed.

Because there are numerous locations where you can set up for anything from an aperitif buffet to the cutting of the cake to formal feasts in the olive grove or by the pool, the park is always subject to inspection. The decision is entirely up to the spouses.

The swimming pool is the most traditional location for a spring wedding in Tuscany. It is flanked by huge concrete areas and a stunning 800 square meter garden. Here, at dusk, you may take in a dreamy vista of Cortona that is enhanced by the candles on the tables and along the poolside.

L'Oliveta is a simple but genuine location where you may experience settings from fairy tales: wicker baskets for an aperitif to the sound of crickets, lights strung amongst the olive trees that resemble bands of fireflies.

The 200 and 100 square meter patios are the most frequently sought for exclusive weddings or entertaining moments. Banquets or simple moments of relaxation can be planned for guests on the north terrace, which offers a distinctive view of Cortona and is close to the swimming pool.

Provided services

The structure's team will assist you in managing and organizing your event, carefully attending to every detail. Everything will carefully follow your instructions, from table management to decoration, from the mis en place to the surrounding area. The building features a parking area with 100 places that blends seamlessly with the entire Borgo complex.

Catering

If it is appreciated by the spouses, Borgo il Melone will be pleased to accept your preferences for setups, scenography, and catering and is willing to offer many alternatives. The arrangement, setup, and high-quality food are the ideal components to crown your wedding reception in this magnificent structure because the most important day can have no restrictions.

Accommodation

If you want to host your guests at Il Borgo or decides to unwind by staying in the building before the big day, you can do it with the help of the 42 beautiful rooms that are available.Experience the most thrilling things at Borgo il Melone.

Address:

Localita il Sodo Case Sparse 38, 52042, Cortona, Italy

Room types

Non-smoking rooms

Suites

Family rooms

Room features

Blackout curtains

Air conditioning

Desk

Housekeeping

Safe

Minibar

Flatscreen TV

Bath / shower

Telephone

Wardrobe / closet

Clothes rack

Private bathrooms

Wake-up service / alarm clock

Complimentary toiletries

Hair dryer

Property amenities

Free parking

Free High Speed Internet (WiFi)

Pool

Free breakfast

Hiking

Horseback riding

Highchairs available

Pets Allowed (Dog / Pet Friendly)

Parking

Wifi

Pool with view

Outdoor pool

Coffee shop

Restaurant

Breakfast available

Breakfast buffet

Vending machine

Car hire

Taxi service

Meeting rooms

Solarium

Baggage storage

Bed and Breakfast

A Bed & Breakfast in Cortona, Italy is a charming and comfortable lodging choice that gives visitors a tailored and comfortable experience.

Here, you may unwind in the conveniences of a home away from home while taking in Cortona's rich culture and natural beauty.

Most Cortona bed & breakfasts have a small number of rooms, making for a more individualized and intimate visit.

The hosts are frequently natives with extensive experience of the neighborhood who are eager to impart their information and offer advice to visitors.

These lodgings provide cozy rooms, frequently decorated in a traditional manner to honor the culture and legacy of the area. Breakfast is typically included in the price and features a delicious variety of locally produced, fresh products to give you a taste of the real flavors of Tuscany.

Being a guest at a Cortona bed & breakfast gives you the chance to interact with the neighborhood because the owners can provide you insider knowledge on the greatest spots for sightseeing, dining, and exploring. A Bed & Breakfast in Cortona offers a warm and friendly ambiance that will make your stay genuinely memorable, whether you're looking for a romantic break or a quiet escape.

The B&B Casa Bellavista

A truely charming bed and breakfast in Tuscany. In the hills between Siena and Perugia in northern Italy, the charmingly rebuilt Tuscan farmhouse known as Casa Bellavista is run by hoteliers Simonetta and Guido, who offer a welcoming, family-style atmosphere and genuine cooking. This eco-friendly, gay-friendly bed and breakfast offers breath-taking views from its cozy, opulent suites or from its vast gardens with pool.

Address:

Case Sparse Creti 40, 52044, Cortona Italy

Room types

Non-smoking rooms

Suites

Family rooms

Room features

Housekeeping

Safe

Bottled water

Minibar

Property amenities

Free parking

Free High Speed Internet (WiFi)

Pool

Free breakfast

Table tennis

Board games / puzzles

Books, DVDs, music for children

Kids' outdoor play equipment

Parking

Wifi

Pool / beach towels

Outdoor pool

Special diet menus

Wine / champagne

Baggage storage

Non-smoking hotel

Outdoor furniture

Sun loungers / beach chairs

Sun terrace

Private check-in / check-   Ironing service
out

La Corte di Ambra B&B

The lovely and elegant B&B La Corte di Ambra, located in
Cortona's old center, is the brainchild of the owners who
insisted on restoring the original residence inside the
opulent Renaissance palace Fierli Petrella. The B&B La
Corte di Ambra in Cortona is refined and exquisite. In this
opulent mansion in the heart of Cortona's historic district,
modern comfort and antique charm coexist together. B&B
La Corte di Ambra offers 2 executive suites, 1 junior suite,
and 2 deluxe rooms, all of which are conveniently located
between Piazza della Repubblica and Piazza Signorelli.

The luxurious B&B enjoys the attentions of traditional
hotel services, for an unforgettable stay with exclusive suite
and room amenities, relax design and corner, depth
reception where organize visits, library and boutique shop,
elevator and an intimate courtyard in the middle of the
noble palace.

The rooms are spacious, and the lobby is furnished with antiques and priceless artwork. Each convenience, including air conditioning, a fireplace, an LED TV, free wifi, a travertine marble bathroom, beautiful linens, and an elegant toiletry kit, is provided in the suites and deluxe rooms.

The breakfast offers a wide variety of sweet and savory delicacies drawn from our preferred selections, showcasing the aromas and flavors of classic Tuscan cuisine. When guests request a special breakfast due to a food allergy or dietary requirement, the owner will arrange for the table to be set in the palace's kitchen on the ground floor. The opulent B&B La Corte di Ambra in the beautiful noble and ancient palace of Cortona is especially made for guests with disabilities to ensure that everyone has a relaxing vacation in Cortona, Tuscany.

Address:
Via Benedetti 23, 52044,
Cortona Italy

Room types

Non-smoking rooms

Suites

Room features

Air conditioning

Minibar

Refrigerator

Flatscreen TV

Free High Speed Internet (WiFi)

Wifi

Hot tub

Free breakfast

Bar / lounge

Non-smoking hotel

Dry cleaning

Laundry service

Breakfast available

B&B Cortona Suite

The Cortona Suite is housed in a 15th-century building and is conveniently situated in Cortona's historic center. It offers elegantly furnished, air-conditioned lodging. The Cortona Suite bed & breakfast offers rooms with fireplaces, flat-screen TVs, and views of Signorelli Square. There is a hairdryer in the private bathroom.

Every day, croissants and cappuccino are served for the Italian breakfast. Items made with gluten can also be prepared. There is free public parking 200 meters away. The distance to Montepulciano is 30 kilometers. It takes 50 minutes to get to Pienza. 300 meters distant is a bus stop that connects to the Camucia di Cortona Train Station.

Address:

Via Benedetti 25, 52044, Cortona Italy

Room types

Non-smoking rooms

Suites

Room features

Air conditioning

Room service

Minibar

Refrigerator

Property amenities

Free High Speed Internet (WiFi)

Wifi

Free breakfast

Pets Allowed (Dog / Pet Friendly)

Non-smoking hotel

B&B Piccolo Hotel

In the heart of Cortona, barely 150 meters from Via Nazionale and Piazza della Repubblica, the Piccolo Hotel B&B debuted in 2012. The hotel has been created to provide visitors with a warm setting for a comfortable and unwinding stay in Cortona. The building is next to the

Hotel San Michele and may provide a continental breakfast to guests upon request (tea, coffee, cappuccino, along with bread, butter, jam, orange juice, and croissants).Despite being in the middle of the town, you can drive within 20 meters of the hotel and, if space permits and upon request, utilize a garage for €20 per day, or park for free in the next public lot 100 meters away.

Address:
Vicolo Petrella 3, 52044, Cortona Italy

Room types
Non-smoking rooms
Family rooms

Room features
Air conditioning
Room service
Minibar

Property amenities
Free High Speed Internet (WiFi)
Hot tub
Free breakfast
Babysitting
Children Activities (Kid / Family Friendly)
Pets Allowed (Dog / Pet Friendly)
Airport transportation

Business Center with
Internet Access
Wifi
Bar / lounge
Breakfast available
Shuttle bus service

Concierge
Non-smoking hotel
Laundry service

Vacation Rental

For visitors seeking a stay that feels like home, a vacation rental in Cortona, Italy is a great option. While touring the lovely town of Cortona, these rentals offer the luxury and convenience of having a completely furnished and equipped space to call your own.

Cozy apartments and roomy villas are just a few of the different sizes and styles of vacation rentals available in Cortona. They frequently offer spectacular views of the surrounding landscapes and are situated in the center of towns or tucked away in lovely countryside.

These accommodations offer all the comforts you require for a peaceful stay, including private bedrooms, nice sitting areas, and well-equipped kitchens. Many also offer extra benefits like outside areas, pools, or gardens so you can unwind and take in the splendor of the Tuscan countryside.

You may fully immerse yourself in the local way of life and culture by selecting a vacation property in Cortona. You can purchase fresh local ingredients at neighboring markets and cook your own meals to get a true sense of Tuscan cuisine. You also have the freedom to make your own plans and take your time discovering the town and its surrounds.

A Cortona vacation rental offers a special chance to experience local life and make priceless memories in this quaint Italian town. A vacation rental in Cortona offers the ideal fusion of luxury, convenience, and authenticity for your trip, whether you're traveling alone, with friends, or as a couple.

Villa Marsili

Greetings from TuscanyAmong the hues of a lovely, giving land offering the grin of a genuinely kind people.Greetings from Cortonaa settlement from the Middle Ages encircled by the Valdichiana's lovely hills Far from clamor and busy schedules...Greetings from Villa Marsili Featuring elegant salons and tastefully decorated, frescoed bedrooms. Welcome to one of the town's most opulent homes' cozy atmosphere.

Address:

San Pietro a Cegliolo, 420, 52044, Cortona Italy

Room types

Bridal suite

Non-smoking rooms

Suites

Good to know

Room features

Air conditioning

Housekeeping

Room service

Safe

Minibar

Flatscreen TV

Property amenities

Free parking

Free High Speed Internet (WiFi)

Pool

Free breakfast

Hiking

Horseback riding

Children Activities (Kid / Family Friendly)

Pets Allowed (Dog / Pet Friendly)

Getting there

Sant Egidio Airport: 31 miles

Peretola Airport: 53 miles

Relais Villa Baldelli

Discover why so many tourists select Relais Villa Baldelli as their lodging choice when they are in Cortona. Offering the perfect balance of affordability, comfort, and convenience, it offers a romantic atmosphere with a number of amenities tailored for visitors just like you.

Relais Villa Baldelli Hotel is a fantastic spot to stay when visiting Cortona because of the nearby attractions like Duomo di Cortona (1.3 mi) and Piazza della Repubblica (1.4 mi).

The Relais Villa Baldelli Hotel offers free wifi and rooms with a flat-screen TV, air conditioning, and a minibar.

Utilize some of the services provided throughout your stay, such as room service, a concierge, and luggage storage. A pool and a free breakfast are also available on site for Relais Villa Baldelli guests. There is free parking for guests arriving by vehicle.

Consider dining at Osteria del Teatro, La Bucaccia da Romano, or Restaurant Il Falconiere if you're searching for an Italian restaurant; they're all conveniently close to Relais Villa Baldelli Hotel.

If you're seeking for activities, check out Meloni di Cortona (0.5 mi) or Agriturismo Il Frantoio (0.5 mi), both of which are close by and well-liked tourist destinations.

Your comfort and happiness are prioritized at Relais Villa Baldelli, and they eagerly await your arrival in Cortona.

Address:

Via Cesare Battisti 13, 52044, Cortona Italy

Room types   Bridal suite

Non-smoking rooms

Suites

Family rooms

Room features

Allergy-free room

Air conditioning

Desk

Housekeeping

Room service

Coffee / tea maker

Cable / satellite TV

Bidet

Safe

Telephone

VIP room facilities

Wardrobe / closet

Bottled water

Laptop safe

Private bathrooms

Wake-up service / alarm clock

Minibar

Electric kettle

Flatscreen TV

Walk-in shower

Whirlpool bathtub

Bath / shower

Complimentary toiletries

Hair dryer

Property amenities

Paid private parking nearby

Free High Speed Internet (WiFi)

Free breakfast

Children's television networks

Highchairs available

Pets Allowed (Dog / Pet Friendly)

Baggage storage

Concierge

Parking

Wifi

Bar / lounge

Breakfast available

Breakfast buffet

Special diet menus

Non-smoking hotel

24-hour front desk

Dry cleaning

Laundry service

Ironing service

Sant Egidio Airport: 29 miles

Peretola Airport: 54 miles

Villa Borgo San Pietro

A former farm from the XVIIth century, Villa Borgo San Pietro is now a lovely hotel with an outdoor pool that has 14 rooms and 5 apartments. Thanks to a thoughtful renovation, the building's new purpose was taken into consideration while yet keeping its historic appearance. The tranquil ambiance and sensation of a Tuscan country house is created by the old well, fruit and olive trees, grass fields, and antique prints, paintings, and furniture.

Address:

Localita San Pietro A Cegliolo, 52044, Cortona Italy

Room types

Non-smoking rooms

Suites

Family rooms

Smoking rooms available

Room features

Air conditioning

Desk

Housekeeping

Room service

Safe

Minibar

Refrigerator

Flatscreen TV

Telephone

Wake-up service / alarm clock

Property amenities

Free parking

Free High Speed Internet (WiFi)

Pool

Free breakfast

Bicycle rental

Hiking

Babysitting

Children Activities (Kid / Family Friendly)

Parking

Wifi

Pool / beach towels

Outdoor pool

Bar / lounge

Breakfast buffet

Table tennis

Pets Allowed (Dog / Pet
Friendly)

Airport transportation

Shuttle bus service

Car hire

Taxi service

BBQ facilities

Baggage storage

Concierge

Mosquito net

Non-smoking hotel

Express check-in / check-
out

Laundry service

Getting there

Sant Egidio Airport: 31 miles

Peretola Airport: 52 miles

Agriturismo Agrisalotto

In the heart of Tuscany, Agrisalotto is an upscale
"agriturismo" and hotel restaurant. Agrisalotto is a simple
yet remarkable restaurant housed in a freshly restored 18th
century "Leopoldina" farm home that nonetheless exudes a
tranquil, rural ambience.A renowned restaurant provides
the chance to sample top-notch Tuscan cuisine with
authentic, traditional meals and paired wines.

They also provide a contemporary swimming pool, a landscape measuring 6,000 square meters, a vineyard, an orchard, a vegetable garden, and a partially covered, lit parking lot.

Address:

S.Caterina Loc. Burcinella, 88, 52044, Cortona Italy

Room features

Room service

Safe

Bottled water

Kitchenette

Property amenities

Free parking

Free High Speed Internet (WiFi)

Pool

Restaurant

Bicycles available

Table tennis

Babysitting

Children Activities (Kid / Family Friendly)

Wifi

Hot tub

Pool / beach towels

Outdoor pool

Breakfast available

Kids' meals

Wine / champagne

Kids' outdoor play equipment

Solarium

BBQ facilities

Outdoor furniture

Sun loungers / beach chairs

24-hour front desk

Express check-in / check-out

Laundry service

Languages spoken

English, French, Italian

Self-serve laundry

Getting there

Sant Egidio Airport: 33 miles

Peretola Airport: 51 miles

CHAPTER 6

S hopping in Cortona, Italy is a fascinating experience that lets tourists explore local culture and find one-of-a-kind items. The town has a wide selection of stores, marketplaces, and boutiques where you may buy a wide range of items and souvenirs.

The handcrafted textiles, leather goods, and ceramics that are produced in Cortona are among its most well-known artisanal goods. The town's talented artisans create exquisite, high-quality objects that are ideal for gifts or as keepsakes. You can examine and buy these artisanal pieces while strolling through the little stores and workshops that line the streets.

Cortona also has hip apparel shops with both regional and global names for individuals who are interested in fashion and style. You can find a variety of selections to fit your style, whether you're seeking for sophisticated Italian fashion or items with a boho flair.

Local speciality stores offer a tempting selection of regional goods that food lovers will love. These shops provide you the chance to sample the flavors of Cortona and bring a piece of Italy home with you. They stock everything from Tuscan wines and olive oils to delectable cheeses and cured meats.

Additionally, Cortona hosts a weekly market where locals and tourists can shop for groceries, regional specialties, clothing, and household items. Its vivacious and colorful ambiance provides a genuine window into the neighborhood's traditions.

Shopping in Cortona is not just about the things you buy; it's also about the experience of absorbing the lively ambiance of the town. Your shopping experience will be enhanced by the welcoming shop owners and artists who are frequently eager to share their expertise and passion for their work.

Shopping in Cortona is a wonderful way to experience the town's rich culture and bring a little bit of it home, whether you're looking for one-of-a-kind mementos, chic clothing, or delicious regional goods.

Souvenir and Gift

Here are some crucial suggestions to bear in mind when shopping for gifts and souvenirs in Cortona:

The majority of Cortona's souvenir and gift stores are open from Monday through Saturday, with some of them closing briefly in the afternoon. The ideal times to go shopping are from 9:00 AM to 1:00 PM, followed by 4:00 PM to 7:30 PM. Please be aware that store hours sometimes change, so it's best to confirm the precise opening times of the shops you intend to visit.

Locally produced crafts and artwork:

- Cortona is well known for its skilled local craftspeople. Look for stores that sell handmade woodwork, fabrics, leather products, and ceramics. These genuine, regionally produced mementos are distinctive and unforgettable.

Delicacies of Food and Wine:

- Look around specialist stores that feature foods and wines from Tuscany. Search for things like regional wines, olive oils, truffle products, and classic Tuscan fare. These gourmet foodstuffs are wonderful presents for food and wine connoisseurs or may be used to recreate the tastes of Cortona at home.

Cultural Memorabilia:

- Look for stores in Cortona that sell books, postcards, prints, or replicas of well-known works of art and landmarks. You can take one of these artifacts home with you to remember Cortona's rich history and culture.

Consider customised souvenirs as a method to make a special and one-of-a-kind keepsake. Find stores that provide customisation options, such as engraved jewelry, monogrammed accessories, or custom apparel. These personalized presents offer a special touch and create priceless treasures.

Shopping Etiquette:

- It is nice to give shops a hearty "buongiorno" (good day) and engage in polite conversation when purchasing presents and souvenirs. Feel free to look around the stores without feeling pressured to buy anything. It's usually appreciated to show gratitude to the shops if you obtain assistance or advise from them.

Supporting Local companies:

- Think about purchasing goods created in Cortona or the nearby region to help local craftsmen and companies. You support the local economy and assist in maintaining traditional workmanship by doing this.

Cash is the most commonly accepted form of payment in smaller establishments, so be sure to have some with you. However, larger retailers and boutiques catering to tourists might also accept credit cards.

You can take a piece of Cortona's beauty and history home by exploring the world of trinkets and gifts there. Enjoy yourself while you browse, immerse yourself in the culture, and discover the ideal souvenirs to remember your trip to this quaint Italian town.

Boutiques and clothing

Here are some crucial suggestions to bear in mind when shopping for clothing and boutique items in Cortona:

The majority of Cortona's fashion stores are open from Monday through Saturday, with some of them closing briefly in the afternoon. The ideal times to go shopping are from 9:00 AM to 1:00 PM, followed by 4:00 PM to 7:30 PM. Please be aware that store hours sometimes change, so it's best to confirm the precise hours of the boutiques you intend to visit.

Fashion and Style:

- Cortona is home to a number of chic stores that provide a range of apparel, accessories, footwear, and jewelry. Discover boutique stores that cater to many types, from classic and elegant to fashionable and contemporary, while exploring the local fashion scene. There is a mixture of domestic and foreign brands, ensuring a wide variety for fashion fans.

Personalized Styling:

- To assist you in finding the ideal dress or accessory, many establishments in Cortona provide personalized styling services. The knowledgeable team can offer style guidance and help you put together a well designed outfit that reflects your personal preferences. Utilize these services to improve your purchasing and find one-of-a-kind items that suit your taste.

Quality and Attention to Detail:

- Cortona's stores frequently place a strong emphasis on craftsmanship and quality. Look for stores that have an emphasis on design, construction, and materials. You can get handcrafted accessories that showcase the commitment to excellence as well as things produced from excellent materials and stunning leather goods.

Explore Italian fashion in Cortona's boutiques to learn more about the latest styles and brands. Given Italy's prominence in the fashion world, you may find a variety of Italian brands and designers in the local boutiques. Cortona provides a window into the world of Italian fashion, showcasing both established fashion houses and up-and-coming designers.

Custom tailoring is available at a few Cortona establishments, allowing you to have clothing made to your precise specifications. This customized touch guarantees a great fit and adds a distinctive aspect to your wardrobe.

Accessories and jewelry:

- Don't forget to browse the boutiques in Cortona's accessory and jewelry selections. You can find a variety of accessories that can easily improve your style and serve as treasured reminders of your trip to Cortona, such as handmade leather purses and artisanal jewelry.

Keep an eye out for fashion-related events and exhibitions that are happening in Cortona. These events frequently feature the newest collections, up-and-coming designers, and cutting-edge trends. Attending these events can offer opportunity to interact with the local fashion scene and a broader understanding of the fashion sector.

Fashion that is ethical and sustainable is promoted by Cortona. Fair trade manufacturing, eco-friendly materials, and ethical sourcing are valued by some shops. By supporting these companies, you can benefit from high-quality, ethically produced clothing while also helping the fashion industry become more sustainable.

Limited Editions and Collaborations:

- Keep up with regional designers, shops, and artists' collaborations. Exclusive limited-edition works that combine fashion and creative expression are frequently the product of these collaborations. By purchasing these one-of-a-kind goods, you support the artistic collaborations taking place in Cortona while also expanding your wardrobe.

Farmers' Markets, and Delis

The specialized shops, farmers' markets, and delis in Cortona provide a pleasurable shopping experience that lets you sample the local fare and find one-of-a-kind goods. What you should know to maximize your buying experience is as follows:

Farmers' Markets:

- Cortona is home to thriving farmers' markets where a variety of recent, regionally grown foods are on display. These markets typically have morning hours beginning at 8 or 9 AM and sell a range of seasonal fruits, vegetables, cheeses, cured meats, and other delights. Engage the neighborhood vendors, try their wares, and bring home the best ingredients for your culinary explorations.

Delis & Gastronomic Shops:

- Explore Cortona's delightful delis and gastronomic shops. A delicious selection of cheeses, cold cuts, olives, truffle products, and other regional specialties are available here. The delis are a haven for foodies looking to experience Cortona's genuine flavors; they frequently open about 10 AM.

Wine and Olive Oil Tastings:

- Cortona is home to a number of specialist shops that let you sample the area's well-known wines and extra virgin olive oils. The tasting will be supervised by knowledgeable professionals who will share insights into the various types and production processes. Take advantage of the chance to get your preferred bottles straight from the makers.

Don't pass up the chance to sample handcrafted pasta and conventional sauces from neighborhood specialty shops. These stores provide an outstanding assortment of pasta shapes, whether you're seeking for traditional pasta variations or one-of-a-kind handcrafted ones.

Specialty shops in Cortona have a variety of gourmet souvenirs that are ideal for giving to food-obsessed friends and family back home. There are many delicious options to share a taste of Cortona with your loved ones, from jars of truffle-infused treats to regional liqueurs and pastries.

Seasonal Offerings:

- Be aware that the season may have an impact on the products' availability. Consider traveling during the height of the harvest, such as the winter olive oil pressing season or the fall truffle season, to experience the flavors at their freshest and most genuine.

Local Recommendations:

- Interact with the populace and business proprietors to learn about their preferred goods and menu suggestions. They frequently want to impart their knowledge and provide helpful advice for discovering Cortona's culinary wonders.

- Organic and sustainable goods are given priority at some specialist shops and farmers' markets in Cortona. In addition to ensuring the best products, patronizing these businesses helps them follow ecologically friendly methods.

Create a personalized gift basket with a carefully chosen assortment of goods from the specialist shops and delis if you're searching for a particular gift or souvenir. This kind deed enables you to create a custom gift that suits your tastes.

Experience Cortona's genuine flavors at its specialized shops, farmers' markets, and delis. Take advantage of the chance to sample, learn about, and take a piece of this enchanting region's culinary legacy home.

Chapter 7

Cortona is a wonderful gastronomic paradise located in the center of Italy when it comes to cuisine and wine. I have a great deal of pride in our area's extensive culinary history as a native. Cortona offers a pleasant voyage for your taste buds, with everything from authentic Tuscan cuisine to superb wines. Here is a quick overview of Cortona's wine and food scene:

Italian food:

Cortona is well known for its genuine Tuscan cuisine, which honors straightforward but tasty dishes prepared using seasonal, nearby ingredients. You'll find a range of classic flavors that capture the spirit of Tuscan cooking, from robust soups like ribollita and pappa al pomodoro to sumptuous meat dishes like bistecca alla fiorentina (Florentine steak) and cinghiale (wild pig).

Local ingredients

Cortona's surroundings are home to a wealth of top-notch ingredients. The local ingredients that enhance the dishes in our trattorias and restaurants include tasty cheeses, fresh vegetables, fragrant herbs, premium olive oil, and artisanal cured meats.

Local Food and Dining Experiences

Cortona cordially invites you to explore its lovely town's thriving culinary scene. Here, you'll find a delectable selection of regional cuisine and culinary experiences that genuinely embody the spirit of our area. Let me give you an overview of some of the highlights:

Osterias and trattorias:

- These inviting places provide a taste of real home-cooked food. Enter and enjoy dishes that highlight the regional flavors of Cortona and are made using ingredients that are locally sourced.

Tuscan Cuisine:

- Enjoy the flavorful cuisine of Tuscany, including the famous Bistecca alla Fiorentina (Florentine steak) and the filling Pappa al Pomodoro (tomato and bread soup). Every morsel is a celebration of regional customs.

Olive Oil:

- Cortona is renowned for producing superb olive oil. Visit nearby oil mills to sip the golden nectar and discover the history of the production of olive oil.

Wine tasting:

- Learn about the renowned local wines, such as the prestigious Vino Nobile di Montepulciano and the refreshing Vernaccia di San Gimignano. For an unforgettable wine tasting experience, visit wineries and vineyards.

Regional Markets

- Investigate the crowded markets where you may discover a wide variety of fresh fruit, local cheeses, cured meats, and aromatic herbs. Engage with regional vendors and bring Cortona's delicacies home.

Cheese of Pecorino:

Enjoy the creamy and tangy Pecorino cheese, which is created from sheep's milk. Visit nearby cheese stores to sample various varieties and discover how artisanal cheese is made.

Agricultural Dining:

- Find restaurants that have an emphasis on farm-to-table eating, where the focus is on using seasonal, fresh products that are sourced directly from nearby farms. On your dish, taste the flavors of the countryside.

Customary Holidays:

- Make arrangements for your trip to coincide with regional cuisine celebrations like the Sagra della Porchetta or the Sagra del Cinghiale. These exciting occasions offer a lively atmosphere for celebration while showcasing regional specialties.

Desserts and ice cream:

- A glass of Vin Santo is the perfect accompaniment to cantucci (almond cookies), a typical Tuscan treat, or the velvety deliciousness of true Italian gelato.

Rural agriturismos

- Discover the appeal of the agriturismos in Cortona, where you can enjoy farm-fresh meals in a rural setting. These places provide a distinctive eating experience rooted on authenticity.

Regional bakeries:

- Visit a nearby bakery first thing in the morning to enjoy the aroma of freshly made breads and pastries. Enjoy a warm cornetto (an Italian croissant) or a piece of old-fashioned tonnolian cake.

Seafood Favorites:

- Despite being an interior city, Cortona offers some of Italy's finest seafood meals. Local eateries frequently provide a variety of seafood delicacies that have been prepared with a hint of Tuscan flair.

Slow Food Principles:

- Acccpt the "slow food" mentality, which emphasizes high standards, environmental protection, and the preservation of traditional culinary practices. Spend some time enjoying each bite and learning about Cortona's extensive culinary history.

We in Cortona are quite proud of our regional cuisine and dining experiences. The secret is to embrace the dishes' simplicity and genuineness and let the flavors carry you away to the heart of Tuscany. Here are some additional suggestions to improve your culinary trip, whether you're dining at a trattoria, visiting the neighborhood markets, or taking a cooking class:

Seasonal Delights:

- Accept that ingredients change with the seasons and savor the new sensations they bring. The varying seasons offer a varied culinary experience, from summer's fresh tomatoes and basil to autumn's earthy mushrooms and truffles.

Food and Wine Pairings

- Investigate the science of wine and food pairing to elevate your dining experience. Local sommeliers and restaurant proprietors can offer advice on the best wines to pair with your meal in order to enhance its characteristics.

Outdoor Dining

- When feasible, choose to eat outside to take advantage of the lovely surroundings. Enjoy your dinner while soaking up Cortona's lively ambiance on lovely terraces or inquaint piazzas.

Wine and cheese pairings:

- To properly enjoy the richness and complexity of Tuscan flavors, indulge in focused cheese and wine tastings. You can learn about the subtleties of various cheeses and wines from local experts, enabling you to identify your own preferences.

Cooking classes and events:

- Keep up with future cooking classes, festivals, and other events going place in Cortona. These gatherings provide special chances to interact with regional chefs, artists, and food lovers.

Locally Made Products:

- By choosing goods with the "KM Zero" or "Prodotti Tipici" labels, you can show your support for regional producers while also ensuring better quality and sustainable production methods.

Traditional desserts from Tuscany:

- Enjoy the sweet side of Tuscan food with classic sweets like ricciarelli, panforte, and tiramisu. These delicious desserts are ideal for satisfying your sweet craving and providing a wonderful way to conclude your dinner.

Culture of Coffee:

- Participate in Cortona's thriving coffee culture. Start your day with a decadent espresso at a neighborhood café, then indulge in the ritual of sipping a caffè macchiato or a foamy cappuccino throughout the day.

Investigating Culinary Mysteries

- Engage the community and start a dialogue about their favorite undiscovered restaurants. They might expose you to undiscovered eateries, family-run trattorias, or specialist stores that provide distinctive culinary experiences.

Observe regional customs:

Respect local traditions when eating out by ordering the customary dishes first (antipasto, primo, secondo, and dolce) and accepting the leisurely pace of meals. This makes it possible for you to completely appreciate the tastes and the sociability of dining in Cortona.

With these tips on Cortona's regional cuisine and dining options, you'll be able to savor the true flavors of our area. Discover the genuine spirit of Cortona through its cuisine as you savor the region's illustrious culinary tradition, indulge in regional specialties, and make priceless memories. Happy eating!

These dishes represent the region of Cortona's rich culinary tradition because they have been handed down through the generations. Let's now discuss some of the famous traditional Tuscan delicacies you just must sample when visiting Cortona:

The Fiorentina steak:

- An absolute pleasure for meat lovers, this classic dish. It comprises of a thick-cut T-bone steak that has been expertly grilled and is simply seasoned with salt, pepper, and extra virgin olive oil. The outcome is a succulent, tender steak with a charred, smokey exterior.

Pomodoro's Pappa:

- This hearty Tuscan staple of tomato and bread soup is homey and hearty. It's a straightforward yet flavorful dish that highlights the value of utilizing high-quality products. It's made with ripe tomatoes, stale bread, garlic, basil, and olive oil.

Ribollita:

- Ribollita is a thick vegetable and bread soup that is another hearty Tuscan meal. Cannellini beans, kale or Swiss chard, carrots, celery, onions, and garlic are frequently used in this dish. The soup is cooked until the flavors converge, and it tastes even better the next day when warmed up.

pici, all'Aglione

- Traditional Tuscan pasta called pici, which resembles thick spaghetti, goes incredibly well with the potent flavors of aglione sauce. The powerful and mildly spiciness of the aglione sauce, which is formed of garlic and tomatoes, pairs beautifully with the homemade pici pasta.

Cacciucco:

- The outstanding seafood from the adjacent coast is highlighted in this Tuscan fish stew. Various types of fish and shellfish are used to make it, and it is cooked in a flavorful tomato-based broth with garlic, onions, and aromatic herbs. The end product is a delicious and cozy dish that perfectly evokes the flavor of the sea.

Panzanella:

- This cool salad is ideal for warm summer days. It includes water-soaked chunks of stale bread with ripe tomatoes, cucumbers, red onions, basil, and liberal amounts of olive oil and vinegar. It's a great approach to take advantage of the seasonal ingredients' freshness.

Cantucci:

- This popular Tuscan dessert is an almond cookie. To get a crisp texture, they are baked twice, and the customary way to eat them is to dip them into Vin Santo, a sweet dessert wine. Crunchy cantucci and sweet wine go together like peaches and cream.

Nonna's' Torta:

- This classic Tuscan delicacy, which translates to "grandmother's cake," is a real treat. It has a buttery shortcrust pastry with a delectable lemon custard within and pine nuts on top. Every mouthful is a divine experience.

Look for these typical Tuscan delicacies when you are in Cortona and experience the flavors that have been adored for ages. These meals will transport you to the heart of Tuscan cuisine whether you eat at a neighborhood trattoria, enroll in a cooking class, or visit the local food markets. Happy eating!

Best Cafes and Restaurants

There are several top restaurants and cafes in this quaint Italian town that can satisfy different tastes and preferences.

Cortona provides a variety of dining options, including both classic Tuscan dishes and cutting-edge culinary inventions. You can choose from a wide variety of businesses that highlight the area's illustrious culinary tradition, ranging from sophisticated bistros to rustic trattorias.

Visit the neighborhood trattorias and osterias if you're looking for true Tuscan cuisine. These welcoming restaurants provide traditional fare made using ingredients obtained nearby. Each taste takes you to the heart of Tuscan cuisine, from hearty pasta dishes to luscious meats and aromatic vegetable-based dishes.

If you're searching for a more modern eating experience, Cortona has a number of eateries that combine classic flavors with cutting-edge cooking methods. Innovative dishes made by talented chefs push the boundaries of flavor and appearance while showcasing the best local ingredients. These culinary gems provide a mix of tastes, textures, and artistic cooking.

Cortona is also home to quaint bakeries and cafes that are ideal for a quick snack or a leisurely rest. Enjoy a cup of freshly made espresso with a choice of sweet pastries, ice cream, or light munchies. These cafes are great places to unwind, people-watch, and take in the neighborhood ambience because of the welcoming mood and pleasant setting.

The restaurants and cafes in Cortona not only serve delicious food, but also frequently have beautiful surroundings. Many provide spectacular panoramas of the town's quaint streets, undulating hills, or picturesque surroundings. You can have your meal in a charming courtyard tucked away in the old center or on a terrace with a view of the valley, depending on your preference.

Be sure to enjoy the conviviality and gracious welcome of the locals as you tour the best eateries and coffee shops in Cortona. Talk to the dedicated chefs and staff, ask for advice, and let them help you choose from the menu. Their expertise and devotion to their work elevate the eating experience and make sure that every visit is one to remember.

The gastronomic environment of Cortona is a mix of age-old tastes, cutting-edge food, and attractive locations. There are many possibilities to satiate your cravings, whether you're looking for modern innovations, traditional foods from Tuscany, or a peaceful cafe to unwind. So, indulge in Cortona's culinary offerings and let your taste senses to travel through Tuscany's delicacies in a memorable way.

Here are a few dining options in Cortona

1. Romano's La Bucaccia

This restaurant offers exquisite, flavorful food and is one of the best venues to learn about Tuscan cuisine in general and Arezzo cuisine in particular. In the historic center, only a few tables are set up along the main street, and the two inside dining rooms have a rustic and romantic atmosphere. Romano, the proprietor, who is amiable and vivacious, deserves special mention because he guarantees amusement in between courses.

Services & Facilities:

Credit card from American Express

Accepting credit and debit cards

Credit card from Diners Club

Credit card from MasterCard

Especially intriguing wine list

Terrace

Visa credit card

Address: Via Ghibellina, 17, 52044 Cortona AR, Italy

Website: www.labucaccia.it

Phone: +39 0575 606039

Opening and closing times

Monday: a holiday

Tuesday-Sunday:

12:30-14:30

19:00-22:30

Café del Teatro

Since 1994, Osteria del Teatro has extended a warm welcome and provided traditional Tuscan cuisine with a variety of delectable dishes. Emiliano Rossi, an accomplished and amiable chef, owns the pleasant and sincere restaurant in Cortona, Italy.

Visit the restaurant for a delicious lunch in Cortona or a special dinner to experience the wonderful Cortona culinary delights! You may savor delicious and sought-after local cuisine at our Cortona restaurant trattoria in a setting that is all its own: a completely rebuilt and brought back to its former glory structure from the sixth century.

Three distinct settings welcome you in a classy and opulent setting: the first room revives the typical elements of the old Tuscan inns, the second is distinguished by a cozy contest, and the third is enriched by priceless frescoes that make your lunch or dinner in Cortona special and intimate.

Address: Via Giuseppe Maffei, 2, 52044 Cortona AR, Italy
Phone: +39 0575 630556

Website: www.osteria-del-teatro.it
Value range

$5- $30

Opening and closing hours:

Mon. – Sunday

12:30 PM - 2:30 PM

7:30 PM - 12:00 AM

Cuisines

Tuscan, Central-Italian, and Italian cuisines

Advanced diet

Gluten-free and vegetarian options

Meals

Lunch, supper, brunch, and late-night meals

Features

Highchairs are available, there is outdoor seating, free wifi, reservations are accepted, private dining is available, alcohol is served, there is a full bar with wine and beer, and table service is available.

2. Cortona Restaurant

Location: Via S. Margherita, 13, 52044 Cortona AR, Italy

Phone: +39 0575 62957

Email: cortonabistrot@gmail.com

Cuisines

Tuscan, Central-Italian, Mediterranean, Italian, Soups

Advanced diet

Options that are vegetarian-friendly, vegan, and gluten-free

Meals

Brunch, lunch, dinner, and beverages

Features

Reservations, outdoor seating, high chairs, wheelchair access, alcohol service (wine and beer), acceptance of Mastercard and Visa, free WiFi, acceptance of credit cards, table service are all available.

4. Bar 500

There are numerous food stands on the streets of Cortona, but Bar 500 is one that is worth going to because of the friendly staff's ability to make you feel at home and the fact that they speak good English. In addition to being flavorful and very Tuscan, the food at Bar 500 is also fairly affordable.

Address: Cortona, Italy, 52044; Via Nazionale 44/46

Website: www.bar500cortona.com

Cuisines

Italian, Bar, Pizza, Tuscan, Central-Italian, and Mediterranean

Options that are vegetarian-friendly, vegan, and gluten-free

Lunch, dinner, brunch, after-hours, and beverages

Takeout, reservations, outdoor seating, wheelchair accessibility, alcohol is served, full bar, credit cards are accepted, table service

CHAPTER 8

Welcome to the exciting world of Cortona's festivals and events, where the city comes to life all year long with vivacious celebrations and cultural gatherings. Cortona, which is located in the heart of Tuscany, has a full calendar of events that highlight the area's rich history and customs.

The Giostra dell'Archidado, a medieval festival that takes place in May, is one of the most well-known occasions in Cortona. With costumed players, jousting contests, music, and theatrical presentations, this captivating spectacle transports you to the Middle Ages. You are transported to a bygone period as the town's streets and squares come to life with humming marketplaces, colorful processions, and parades.

The Tuscan Sun Festival, an annual festival of music, art, and culture, is another important event on the calendar. World-class performers, musicians, and artists are drawn to this international festival, captivating audiences with their skill and originality. The Tuscan Sun Festival presents a wide variety of cultural activities set against the breathtaking scenery of Cortona, from classical concerts to cutting-edge acts.

A number of gastronomic celebrations showcasing the area's culinary traditions are also held in Cortona. A meat lover's delight, the Sagra della Bistecca, which takes place in August, features juicy steaks that have been expertly cooked and served with a side of regional specialties. Visitors to this food festival come together to enjoy the flavors of Tuscany and the famed cuisine of the area, making it a veritable feast for the senses.

Cortona celebrates its creative heritage all year long with exhibitions, gallery openings, and cultural activities. The town's museums and galleries display the creations of regional and worldwide artists, providing a window into the active art scene. Cortona's cultural events offer a stage for artistic expression and appreciation, from modern works of art to timeless treasures.

You'll see that the people of Cortona have a strong feeling of community and pride as you explore the festivals and events held there. Visitors are cordially welcomed to join in the celebrations and fully immerse themselves in the local customs, which creates a memorable experience for them.

The festivals and events held in Cortona offer an enthralling fusion of gastronomy, history, art, and music. Cortona's calendar is packed with opportunities to experience the dynamic character of this delightful Tuscan town, whether you're drawn to medieval pageantry, cultural performances, or culinary pleasures. Make a note of these events in your calendar and come celebrate Cortona's rich cultural legacy while making lifelong memories.

Festival Mix Cortona

We're glad you're here at the exciting Cortona Mix Festival, a yearly celebration of the arts, music, and cultural enlightenment. This spectacular occasion takes place in July and draws guests from near and far to enjoy a combination of inspiration and creativity.

- You can get lost in a wide variety of artistic expressions while attending the Cortona Mix Festival. The festival offers a compelling lineup of performances, installations, and exhibitions that cover a range of genres and media. You'll see provocative pieces by well-known artists, both local and foreign, in everything from contemporary art to multimedia performances.

The Cortona Mix Festival offers an outstanding musical program in addition to visual arts. Get ready to be mesmerized by live performances, concerts, and DJ sets that feature a diverse range of genres, from jazz to techno, classical to modern. The festival's musical program aims to enthrall your senses and produce an environment you won't soon forget.

Things to do

- The Cortona Mix Festival features a variety of participatory activities in addition to exhibitions and music. Participate in seminars and workshops conducted by accomplished artists to discover your own creative potential and pick up new skills. Participate in debates and seminars that explore the nexus between art, culture, and society to stimulate thought and dialogue.

Site-specific artworks and performances are also part of the festival, which expands its reach beyond conventional venues to include all of Cortona. Discover the charming alleys and squares of the town, where art melds with the urban environment to create unexpected artistic encounters at every turn.

Explore the Cortona Mix Festival to learn about a world of creative opportunities. Participate in the exhibits, watch engaging performances, and savor the vivacious cultural ambiance. During this extraordinary event, immerse yourself in thought-provoking discussions, broaden your artistic horizons, and embrace the creative spirit that permeates Cortona.

Make a note of the Cortona Mix Festival for July on your calendars and get ready to be inspired. This festival promises to spark your imagination and create a lasting impact, whether you're an experienced art fan or simply keen to explore new cultural experiences. Join other art enthusiasts, interact with accomplished artists, and allow the Cortona Mix Festival lead you on a creative, inspirational, and educational trip.

Joust in Archidado

Discover the intriguing Archidado Joust, a spectacular annual event that takes place in Cortona. This historical reenactment, which takes place in May, brings to life the customs and chivalry of medieval times.

What to see

- You may see a stunning spectacle as costumed competitors engage in a contest of skill and accuracy during the Archidado Joust. The competition recreates the old rivalry between the four districts of the city, which are each represented by gallant jousters. They target the target with the greatest accuracy while mounted on horses and carrying lances, showcasing their riding skills and seeking for victory.

The event's climax, the jousting competition, draws large throngs of spectators who enthusiastically support their preferred district. As the jousters race towards the target and display their bravery and ability, the air is charged with anticipation and excitement. As they compete to win points for their district and claim the coveted title of Archidado, observe the tension.

Things to do

- The Archidado Joust offers a variety of other activities and attractions in addition to the joust itself. Discover the bustling medieval market where artisans, craftspeople, and vendors are presenting their goods. Enjoy local specialties while strolling among the busy vendors and soaking in the lively ambience of a bygone age.

Don't miss the vibrant historical procession where participants parade through Cortona's streets dressed in traditional attire. Observe the rich symbolism and elaborate patterns of their clothing to learn more about the culture and traditions of the area.

Participate in the festivities to fully experience the joyous atmosphere. Enjoy the aromas of regional cuisine, participate in age-old games and activities, and soak up the atmosphere of fellowship. Stunning musical and dance performances are also available, further enhancing the Archidado Joust's cultural diversity.

The Archidado Joust in Cortona is a must-see event whether you're a history buff, a follower of medieval legend, or just looking for a distinctive cultural experience. You may experience a fully immersive trip into the past at this event, where you can see how people lived in the past. So, make a note of this exciting event in May on your calendars and get ready to be whisked away to a period of knights, pageantry, and tough rivalry.

Come to Cortona for the lively Arts & Crafts Festival, a celebration of artistic expression and innovation. This event, which takes place in August, displays the enormous ability and skill of regional and worldwide artists.

What to see

- The streets of Cortona come alive with a variety of artistic exhibits and exhibitions during the Arts and Crafts festival. Explore the quaint squares and winding streets to discover the diverse selection of artwork, including paintings, sculptures, ceramics, textiles, and more. Admire the artists' talent and originality as they display their one-of-a-kind works, each one a monument to their creative vision.

Things to do

- The festival presents a superb chance to become fully immersed in the world of art. Enjoy the variety of styles and techniques on exhibit as you leisurely browse the numerous galleries and stalls. Talk to the artists directly to acquire insight into their thinking process and sources of inspiration.

The event includes live performances and interactive workshops in addition to visual arts. Take in musical concerts, dramatic productions, and dance recitals that highlight the range of local talent. Participate in practical classes where you can improve your present talents or pick up new ones while being guided by professional artists.

The chance to buy one-of-a-kind and handcrafted things straight from the artists is one of the festival's attractions. You will find a broad variety of treasures to select from, whether it's a painting that catches your heart, a piece of jewelry that matches your style, or a wonderfully produced ceramic item for your house. Support regional artists and bring home a unique gift with sentimental value.

The festival offers cultural activities and culinary experiences in addition to exhibitions and workshops. Enjoy the delectable local cuisine, try some local wines, and soak up the joyous spirit that fills the streets. Engage with other art fans, exchange stories, and create bonds that honor the wonder of imagination.

The Cortona Arts & Crafts Festival honors skill, zeal, and creative expression. It provides a special chance to become lost in the world of art, meet new artists, and take in the beauty that is all around us. So, put this amazing event in August on your calendar and be ready to be mesmerized by the diversity of artistic endeavors.

Authentic Handicrafts

Discover the captivating Traditional Handicrafts Festival in Cortona, which honors time-honored skills and cultural heritage. This yearly occasion takes place in July and attracts guests from near and far to see the craftsmanship of traditional artisans.

What to see

- You will have the chance to see the rebirth and preservation of age-old skills and practices at the Traditional Handicrafts Festival. Take a stroll through the busy streets decorated with colorful stalls and exhibits that feature a variety of traditional crafts, including ceramics, weaving, carpentry, and leathercraft.

Things to do

- Explore the intricately created products on offer and let the rich tapestry of artisanal crafts envelop you. Each element of the region's cultural history, from delicate ceramics decorated with elaborate designs to painstakingly carved wooden sculptures, tells a narrative. As the artists demonstrate their techniques and give an insight into their creative process, be in awe of their talent and passion.

The event provides an opportunity to speak with the artists directly, gaining insights into their work and the customs that have been passed down through the years. Take part in discussions with these gifted people to discover more about the background and significance of their works. Take the chance to ask them questions, value their knowledge, and learn more about the cultural relevance of traditional handicrafts.

The Traditional Handicrafts Festival includes interactive seminars and demonstrations in addition to showcasing the craftsmanship. Attend courses run by knowledgeable artisans to learn the fundamentals of time-honored methods and produce your own original works of art. Explore the technique of pottery-making, try your hand at leather tooling, or study handweaving with the help of skilled artisans.

The event is a celebration of the neighborhood's culture and customs in addition to the crafts themselves. Experience live musical performances, ethnic dances, and cultural exhibitions that capture the essence of Cortona's history. Enjoy regional cuisine that has been crafted over many years, and experience the traditional treats that have become synonymous with the area.

An enthralling display of talent, originality, and cultural legacy is the Traditional Handicrafts Festival. It invites you to travel back in time and take in the elegance and skill of conventional arts. So, put this exciting event in July on your calendar and get ready to explore the world of traditional handicrafts, where the past comes to life and imagination has no limitations.

Chapter 9

An fantastic starting point for exploring the area and going on exciting day trips is Cortona. You'll have the chance to find lovely villages, breathtaking scenery, and cultural treasures nearby thanks to its advantageous position and simple access to transportation.

Travel outside of Cortona to experience the mesmerizing splendor of the Tuscan countryside. View the magnificent vistas studded with olive trees, vineyards, and rolling hills. Admire the quaint hilltop communities with their stories to tell and a sense of being locked in time.

Siena

Exploring the historical allure and cultural diversity of this alluring city on a day trip from Cortona is a rewarding experience. The following information will help you organize your trip:

Distance:

Cortona and Siena are separated by around 70 kilometers.

Time:

Depending on traffic and the route taken, it takes between 1.5 and 2 hours to go from Cortona to Siena.

What to see:

- Siena is highly known for its intact medieval buildings and historical sites. Be sure to check out the magnificent Il Duomo, or Siena Cathedral, with its complex exterior and exquisite interior. Discover the Piazza del Campo, the city's main square, and take in the views of the Torre del Mangia and Palazzo Pubblico. Don't pass up the chance to explore the ancient district's winding lanes and take in the distinctive ambiance.

Transport technique:

- Driving is the most practical means of transportation from Cortona to Siena. You have the option of driving your own car or renting one. As an alternative, there are public transit choices including buses and trains that provide a more leisurely trip without the inconvenience of parking.

Transportation costs:

- Depending on the mode of transportation, different methods have different costs. If you own a car, factor in costs like gas and tolls. If you decide to use public transportation, one-way bus or rail tickets normally cost between €10 and €20 per person.

As you discover Siena's outstanding sights, savor delectable regional cuisine, and meander through its quaint streets, immerse yourself in its beauty and history. A day excursion from Cortona to Siena guarantees an outstanding experience that will leave you with priceless memories, whether you are mesmerized by the stunning architecture or intrigued by the city's cultural legacy.

Florence

A universe of artistic, historical, and architectural delights can be discovered by traveling to Florence in a single day from Cortona. The important information for organizing your trip is as follows:

Distance:

Cortona and Florence are separated by around 120 kilometers.

Time:

Depending on traffic and the route taken, the drive from Cortona to Florence takes between 1.5 and 2 hours.

What to see:

- There are several famous sites and works of art in Florence. Don't miss the majestic Florence Cathedral, Il Duomo, with its magnificent Brunelleschi-designed dome. Investigate the Uffizi Gallery, which has a large collection of Renaissance artwork by artists including Botticelli, Leonardo da Vinci, and Michelangelo. Discover the splendor of Piazza della Signoria, home to the Palazzo Vecchio and a number of statues, and the Ponte Vecchio, a charming bridge surrounded by businesses.

Transport technique:

- Driving is the most practical means of transportation from Cortona to Florence. You may use your own vehicle or a day-use automobile rental. As an alternative, there are public transportation choices including trains and buses that provide a more leisurely trip without the trouble of finding parking in Florence's city center.

Transportation costs:

- Depending on the mode of transportation, different methods have different costs. If you drive your own vehicle, factor in costs like gas and parking. If you decide to use public transportation, one-way train tickets normally cost between €10 and €20 per person.

Enjoy the culinary delights of Florence while strolling through its medieval streets, seeing its renowned museums, and immersing yourself in the aesthetic and cultural glories of the city. Florence offers a unique experience that will astound you, from the classic Renaissance architecture to the bustling local markets.

Perugia

You can explore Perugia's attractions and learn about its extensive cultural legacy by taking a day excursion from Cortona there. The important information for organizing your trip is as follows:

Distance:

Cortona and Perugia are separated by about 60 kilometers.

Time:

Depending on traffic and the route taken, the trip from Cortona to Perugia takes between one and one and a half hours.

What to see:

- There are numerous landmarks in Perugia that reflect its historical importance. Discover the majestic Palazzo dei Priori, which houses the National Gallery of Umbria, in Perugia's ancient center. View the Perugia Cathedral, a masterpiece of architecture, from the famed Fontana Maggiore on Piazza IV Novembre. Don't pass up the opportunity to explore secret passageways, wander through the city's lovely streets, and indulge in regional food.

Transport technique:

- Driving is the most practical means of transportation from Cortona to Perugia. You have the option of driving your own car or renting one. Additionally, there are options for public transit, including buses and trains, which offer a comfortable journey and do away with the trouble of parking.

Transportation costs:

- Depending on the mode of transportation, the cost may change. If you decide to drive, keep costs like gas and tolls in mind. Tickets for public transportation, such buses or trains, normally cost between €5 and €20 per person, one trip.

Explore Perugia's fascinating sights, take in the lively atmosphere, and sample the regional cuisine as you immerse yourself in its beauty and history. A day excursion from Cortona to Perugia guarantees a memorable experience full of discoveries and joys, whether you're attracted by the city's artistic past or intrigued by its cultural attractions.

Amelia

A day journey from Cortona to Amelia enables you to discover the charm and beauty of this quaint town. The following information will help you organize your trip:

Distance:

Cortona and Amelia are separated by around 90 kilometers.

Time:

Depending on the route taken and the amount of traffic, the trip from Cortona to Amelia takes between 1.5 and 2 hours.

What to see:

- The well-preserved medieval walls and Amelia's extensive archaeological history have made the city famous. Discover the city's historic core, which is home to sights like the impressive Porta Romana, the age-old Roman cisterns known as "la Domus del Mitreo," and the splendid Cathedral of Amelia. Discover the town's lovely squares and attractive corners by taking a leisurely stroll through its gorgeous streets.

Transport technique:

- Driving is the most practical means of transportation from Cortona to Amelia. You have the option of driving your own car or renting one. As an alternative, there are public transportation options like buses and trains that guarantee a comfortable trip and do away with the need to find parking.

- Depending on the mode of transportation, the cost may change. If you decide to drive, factor in costs like gas and tolls. Tickets for public transportation, such buses or trains, normally cost between €10 and €20 per person, one trip.

Explore Amelia's historical gems, take in the local culture, and appreciate the medieval ambiance as you take in the city's genuine Italian flavor. A day excursion from Cortona to Amelia ensures that you will have a wonderful experience that is rich in beauty and discovery, whether you are captivated by the town's archaeological monuments or enchanted by its architectural marvels.

CHAPTER 10

Practical Information

It's crucial to have access to useful knowledge that can improve your experience and make your trip to Cortona go well. The following is some useful information for your trip to Cortona:

Options for Accommodation

You can find a wide range of lodging alternatives in Cortona to match your interests and price range. Let me give you some details about the various types of lodging Cortona has to offer:

Hotels:

Cortona is home to a variety of hotels, from opulent resorts to inviting inns. These hotels provide guests with welcoming accommodations, courteous service, and conveniences like bars, restaurants, and swimming pools. Some hotels are situated in the town's historic core, allowing you to fully experience the charm and aura of the place.

B&Bs (bed and breakfasts):

In Cortona, B&Bs provide a more individualized and private experience. These little lodgings are frequently managed by families and offer nice rooms with comfortable beds. Many B&Bs offer a satisfying breakfast to get your day off to a good start, and the proprietors are frequently informed about the neighborhood and can offer useful advice.

Rentals for holidays:

For those looking for a home away from home, renting a villa, condo, or country house is a popular choice. A variety of vacation rentals are available in Cortona to accommodate various group sizes and tastes. These accommodations give you the autonomy and flexibility to set your own schedule while taking use of the conveniences of a fully furnished room.

Agriturismo:

Consider vacationing at an agriturismo for a distinctive experience. The majority of these rural lodgings are functioning farms or country estates with guest rooms or flats. You can take in the peace and quiet of the countryside, savor farm-to-table cuisine, and even get involved in farm chores.

Boarding houses and inns:

Additionally, Cortona features guesthouses and inns that offer cozy lodging at a more reasonable cost. These accommodations provide tidy, basic lodging that is ideal for guests that value affordability while yet wanting a pleasurable stay.

Think about facilities, closeness to attractions or public transit, and location when selecting your lodging. To ensure your preferred choice, it is important to make reservations in advance, especially during the busiest travel times. Cortona provides a variety of lodging choices to suit your preferences and make your time in the town genuinely unforgettable, whether you prefer the comfort of a B&B, the luxury of a hotel, or the independence of a vacation rental.

Cortona's transportation system

You have a number of easy options for getting around Cortona and its surrounds when it comes to transportation.

Walking:

Cortona is a little town with a lovely medieval center that is easily accessible on foot. You can experience the local atmosphere, find hidden treasures, and get to many attractions in the town itself by strolling through the little streets and alleyways.

Using Public Transit:

A dependable bus network connects Cortona to adjacent towns and cities. Local bus services offer transportation to adjacent locations, including close-by train stations and well-known tourist attractions. Always verify the bus schedules before making travel arrangements.

Taxis:

In Cortona, taxis are readily available and can be a practical means of transportation, particularly if you want a door-to-door service. In the town center, taxi stands can be found.

You can also make arrangements for a pickup from a nearby service.

Auto rental

A smart choice if you want the independence to go at your own leisure is to rent a car. There are car rental companies in Cortona where you can pick from a choice of automobiles. You have the freedom to explore surrounding towns, attractions, and the breathtaking Tuscan countryside if you have a car.

Bicycles:

Cycling lovers will love the lovely landscapes that Cortona and its surroundings have to offer. From nearby stores, you may rent bicycles and take beautiful rides through the countryside, vineyards, and olive orchards. You may explore the region's splendor at a leisurely pace while cycling.

Presented Tours:

Joining guided tours is an additional means of getting around and visiting the sights. These trips frequently include transportation, making it simple to visit well-known sights and attractions in and around Cortona. Whether it's a wine tour, a cultural outing, or a historical investigation, guided excursions provide a planned and educational method to explore the area.

Don't forget to consider your transportation options based on your interests and agenda. Some attractions could necessitate the use of multiple transit options. If you opt to rent a car, it's also crucial to look into any unique rules or parking requirements. Use Cortona's transportation choices to your advantage to easily explore the city and its surrounds and get the most out of your trip.

Local Advice:

I advise visiting the countryside in the early morning or late afternoon when it's cooler outside and the lighting is best for taking pictures of the scenery. To make sure you stay on course and don't miss any hidden jewels along the road, don't forget to bring a map or utilize a navigation software.

Cycling in Cortona enables you to take in the breathtaking scenery of Tuscany, breathe in the fresh air, and discover the area's natural beauty at your own leisure. Biking offers a distinctive and satisfying way to explore the charm of Cortona and its environs, whether you opt for a leisurely ride through the countryside or take on a difficult course.

Tips for health and safety

Here are some crucial health and safety advice you should have in mind while visiting Cortona:

Stay hydrated

- It's crucial to drink enough of water because Cortona's summers may be quite hot and dry. Always keep a bottle of water on hand, and be sure to sip on it frequently, especially if you're out touring the city or doing outdoor activities.

Use Sunscreen

- In Cortona, the sun can be very strong, especially when the day is at its brightest. Put on sunscreen with a high SPF, a hat, sunglasses, and light clothing that covers your skin to shield yourself from UV rays. Whenever feasible, seek shade, especially when it's scorching outside.

Personal safety techniques

- Cortona is a relatively safe town, although it's a good idea to exercise caution as you would anywhere new. Keep an eye on your possessions and keep expensive goods hidden when not in use. When out at night, stick to crowded, well-lit streets and follow your instincts regarding your personal safety.

Medical Resources

- Make sure you are familiar with where the medical facilities are in Cortona. Know the location of the closest hospital, clinic, or pharmacy in case of any medical emergencies. Keep crucial phone numbers handy, such as those for your embassy and the emergency services.

Travel Protection

- It is advised to obtain travel insurance that provides coverage for unforeseen circumstances such as medical emergencies and trip cancellations. Before leaving, check your policy to make sure it covers your needs.

Numerals for emergencies

- Save the phone numbers for your local police, fire department, ambulance service, and your embassy or consulate under "emergency numbers." You will always have access to these numbers in case of an emergency.

Water and Food Safety

- Although Cortona has some fantastic restaurants, you must make sure the food and water you eat are safe. utilize a water purifying system or bottled water, as appropriate. When going out to eat, pick reputed restaurants that follow food safety regulations.

Language support

- Despite the fact that most Cortona residents understand English, it never hurts to brush up on a few fundamental Italian words. This can promote communication and demonstrate sensitivity to regional customs.

Awareness of the weather

- Keep an eye on the weather while you're there. Cortona's climate varies throughout the year, so bring the right clothes and accessories for the time of year you'll be there. Before scheduling any outdoor activities, check the weather forecast and be ready for alterations in the weather.

You may guarantee a comfortable and pleasurable trip to Cortona by according to these safety and health recommendations.

Dining

- For different price ranges, Cortona provides a variety of dining options. Investigate neighborhood trattorias, pizzerias, and cafés that serve moderately priced food to save money on meals. Look for daily discounts or fixed-price lunch menus, which are frequently more affordable than supper selections. To have a low-cost supper, think of packing a picnic in one of Cortona's charming parks or squares with delectable local fare from markets.

Regional Markets

- Visit the neighborhood markets in Cortona, like the weekly farmers' market, to get affordable local goods and fresh produce. If your lodging has a kitchenette, you may stock up on supplies for a picnic or even cook your meals.

Daily Budget

You can enjoy Cortona's rich history and culture without going broke thanks to the town's many free or inexpensive activities. Visit the churches, museums, and historical sites in the community that offer entry costs that are reasonable or discounted. Take leisurely strolls through Cortona's streets, parks, and surrounding countryside to take in the city's picturesque charm.

Make a plan

To minimize unforeseen costs or impulsive purchases, do your research and make your plans in advance. For attractions, events, or guided tours, look for discounted tickets, discounts, or special offers. Since they frequently provide free or inexpensive entertainment, find out if any festivals or events are taking place during your visit.

Water and food

To stay hydrated all day, have a reusable water bottle with you. Use public water fountains to refill it, or inquire if tap water is available at cafés and restaurants. Packing some snacks like fruits, energy bars, or almonds might help you avoid making impulsive purchases between meals and reduce hunger.

Souvenirs

Look around your neighborhood for specialty shops, artisanal studios, or markets where you can locate one-of-a-kind, reasonably priced goods if you're wanting to buy mementos. Consider buying handmade items that represent Cortona's history and tradition to support the local artists and craftspeople.

Financial Apps

To manage your everyday expenditures, think about using budgeting apps or maintaining a notepad of your receipts. This might assist you in sticking to your spending plan and locating areas where you can make necessary cuts.

Tipping

Although not as common in Cortona as it is in some other nations, tips are nonetheless expected when given for exceptional service. Whether a service charge is not already included in your statement, check to see whether one is and, if not, consider giving a token tip of a few euros.

You may make the most of your time in Cortona while minimizing your spending by adhering to these daily budgeting advice. Keep in mind that it's usually a good idea to have some extra money on hand for unforeseen costs or unique experiences you may have while visiting. To plan a great and reasonable trip, take use of your time in Cortona while being cautious of your spending limit.

Emergency Contacts

Knowing the correct emergency phone numbers is essential for travelers in Cortona, Italy, in case of any unanticipated circumstances. The following are the numbers to remember in case of an emergency:

- **Medicine Emergencies:**

To contact the Emergency Medical Service (Servizio di Emergenza Sanitaria), phone 118 in the event of a medical emergency. They'll send an ambulance right away to your location.

- Police and legal authorities

Dial 113 to reach the Polizia di Stato (State Police) in case of an emergency requiring police assistance, to report a crime, or to ask for help. They will offer the assistance and direction required.

- Department of Fire

To contact the Vigili del Fuoco (Fire Department) in case of a fire or any other emergency requiring immediate firefighting help, phone 115. They will act quickly to deal with the matter.

Remember that these emergency lines are only to be used in dire circumstances. You can get help from tourist information centers in Cortona, the neighborhood police station, or the embassy or consulate of your country for non-emergency questions or general assistance.

When traveling, it's important to put your safety and wellbeing first. Having access to reliable emergency numbers guarantees that, should the need arise, you can get the assistance and support you require without delay.

It's good to learn the local language and manners before traveling to Cortona as a visitor to ensure a nice and courteous trip. Here are some helpful linguistic and cultural pointers:

Language: Italian is the official language of Italy. While English may be used in tourist areas, it's still a good idea to learn a few fundamental Italian expressions. Visitors that make an attempt to communicate with the locals in their language are appreciated. These words and phrases are helpful:

It is customary to say "buonasera" (good evening) and "buongiorno" (good morning).

When speaking with locals, use the courteous expressions "per favore" (please) and "grazie" (thank you).

Both "mi dispiace" (I'm sorry) and "mi scusi" can be used to express regret or draw attention to oneself.

Respect and Courtesy: In Italy, courtesies and respect are valued. It's polite to smile and make eye contact while greeting people in the community. Be considerate of others' personal space and refrain from being too rowdy or loud in public.

Although there isn't a set dress code in Cortona, it's best to wear modest clothing when entering churches, temples, or other formal buildings. For touring the town's cobblestone streets, it's also a good idea to wear comfy shoes.

Table manners are crucial, such as waiting for everyone to be served before eating, keeping your hands on the table (but not your elbows), and using utensils instead of your hands unless it's a specific finger food, according to Cortona's customs.

Tipping: In Italy, a service fee (coperto) that covers table service is frequently included in the bill. However, it's customary to give an extra little tip for particularly good service. You can leave a tip of between 5 and 10 percent of the total amount, or you can round up the sum.

Respect local traditions and customs by being culturally sensitive. When visiting holy locations, be aware of dressing modestly and refrain from inappropriate behavior or loud talks. Additionally, follow authorized smoking places and don't litter.

Italians are renowned for their expressive gestures and body language in nonverbal communication. While some gestures may be different from those in other cultures, it's crucial to grasp their meanings to prevent any miscommunications.

Keep in mind that by adopting local ways of life, you can have a more authentic cultural experience in Cortona. The people there will value your efforts, and it can result in deeper connections with them while you're there.

Useful phrase

As a tourist in Cortona, it can be helpful to learn some useful phrases to navigate your way around the town and communicate with the locals. Here are a few practical phrases to keep in mind:

Greetings:

"Buongiorno" - Good morning

"Buonasera" - Good evening

"Ciao" - Hello/Goodbye (informal)

Basic Expressions:

"Per favore" - Please

"Grazie" - Thank you

"Prego" - You're welcome

"Mi scusi" - Excuse me

"Mi dispiace" - I'm sorry

Asking for Help:

"Parla inglese?" - Do you speak English?

"Mi può aiutare, per favore?" - Can you help me, please?

"Dov'è...?" - Where is...?

"Posso avere un consiglio?" - Can I have some advice?

Ordering Food and Drinks:

"Un tavolo per uno/due, per favore" - A table for one/two, please

"Posso avere il menù?" - Can I have the menu?

"Vorrei ordinare..." - I would like to order...

"Un bicchiere di vino, per favore" - A glass of wine, please

"Il conto, per favore" - The bill, please

Getting Around:

"Dov'è la stazione dei treni/autobus?" - Where is the train/bus station?

"Quanto costa un biglietto per...?" - How much is a ticket to...?

"A che ora parte il treno/autobus per...?" - What time does the train/bus to... leave?

Shopping:

"Quanto costa?" - How much does it cost?

"Posso provarlo?" - Can I try it on?

"Accettate carte di credito?" - Do you accept credit cards?

"Dove posso trovare...?" - Where can I find...?

Remember, even attempting to speak a few phrases in Italian shows respect and appreciation for the local culture. The locals will likely be more helpful and welcoming if you make an effort to communicate with them in their language.

Chapter 11

To make the most of your time in this picturesque town, it's beneficial to prepare your itinerary and transport arrangements before your trip to Cortona. Here are some ideas for itineraries to take into account:

One-Day Highlights in Cortona:

Morning:

- Investigate Cortona's ancient center to start the day. Visit Piazza della Repubblica, the city's central plaza, and take in the magnificent Palazzo Comunale and Clock Tower.

Mid-Morning:

- View the collection of religious artwork and artifacts at the Museo Diocesano.

Lunch:

- Indulge in a leisurely meal of authentic Tuscan fare at a nearby trattoria.

Afternoon:

- Explore the historic city walls for sweeping views of the surrounding landscape. Discover the town's historical past by visiting the Etruscan Academy Museum.

Evening:

- Attend a live play at the Teatro Signorelli or take in a leisurely dinner with regional specialties at one of the neighborhood restaurants.

Exploring Cortona for Three Days:

Day 1:

Morning:

- Discover Cortona's historic sites, such as the Basilica of Santa Margherita and the Cathedral of Santa Maria Assunta.

Afternoon:

- Visit the adjacent Lake Trasimeno on a day trip. Visit the charming town of Passignano sul Trasimeno, take a leisurely boat ride, and unwind on the lake's beaches.

Evening:

- Return to Cortona and enjoy a great meal at a neighborhood osteria.

Day 2:

Morning:

- Visit nearby Montepulciano, which is renowned for its fine wines, on a day trip. Explore the quaint town, visit wineries, and sample regional wines.

Afternoon:

- Visit the Museo dell'Accademia Etrusca & della Città di Cortona when you go back to Cortona to discover more about the Etruscan culture.

Evening:

- At one of the neighborhood restaurants, treat your significant other to a candlelit meal and a glass of local wine.

Day 3:

Morning:

- Go on a beautiful drive to the charming village of Arezzo. Visit the Basilica of San Francesco, meander around the quaint streets, and explore the ancient district.

Afternoon:

- After arriving back in Cortona, spend the day shopping for one-of-a-kind presents and souvenirs at the neighborhood stores and boutiques.

Evening:

- Enjoy a meal with genuine Tuscan cuisine at a Cortona trattoria.

Cortona and Surroundings for a Week:

Day 1-3:

- Stick to the above-mentioned Three-Day Cortona Exploration schedule.

Day 4–7:

- Tour the surrounding Tuscan hilltop communities of Montalcino, Pienza, and San Gimignano. Visit wineries, sample world-class wines, and become fully immersed in these towns' rich cultural legacy.

Visit Florence, the birthplace of the Renaissance, for the day. Visit famous sites like the Ponte Vecchio, Uffizi Gallery, and Duomo.

Discover the stunning Val d'Orcia region, renowned for its picturesque scenery, quaint villages, and hot springs.

Enjoy the tranquillity of the surroundings while taking leisurely walks, seeing nearby farms, and relaxing in the Tuscan countryside.

Don't forget to adjust your itinerary to reflect your interests and the amount of time you have available. You can fully acquaint yourself with the splendor and culture of Tuscany by exploring Cortona and its surrounds, which are rich in experiences and attractions.

Local Wine:

Cortona is situated in Tuscany, a region renowned around the world for its superb wines. Take the chance to purchase a few bottles of regional wine, such as a bold red Chianti or a fresh Vernaccia. Find the ideal bottle to enjoy at home or to give as a present by visiting one of the town's enotecas (wine stores) or vineyards.

Avocado Oil:

Additionally well-known is Tuscany's premium olive oil. Look for bottles of extra virgin olive oil produced using olives from nearby orchards. Tuscan olive oil is a flexible and delectable complement to any cuisine because of its rich, fruity flavor and smooth texture. Olive oil is available in specialty stores, or for a genuinely authentic experience, head to a nearby olive oil mill.

Custom-made ceramics:

Particularly in pottery, Cortona is renowned for its traditional artistry. Discover gorgeous hand-painted ceramics, from ornamental plates and bowls to one-of-a-kind tiles and vases, by perusing the neighborhood artisan shops and galleries. These items make beautiful home décor or considerate gifts.

Quality Leather:

Cortona provides a selection of the high-quality leather goods that are famously produced in Italy. Look for leather accessories like belts, wallets, handbags, and even specially crafted shoes. High-quality, fashionable, and long-lasting items are guaranteed thanks to the local craftsmanship.

Prints and artwork:

Cortona has historically served as a source of creativity for artists, and you can visit a number of galleries to see pieces created by regional painters, sculptors, and photographers. Think of getting a piece of artwork or a print that perfectly depicts Cortona's beauty and spirit. It will act as a priceless remembrance of your time spent in the town.

Tuscan cuisine's specialties:

Rich agricultural land and vineyards surround Cortona, providing a wide range of culinary delicacies. Look for containers of regional honey, truffles or items infused with them, containers of pickled vegetables, or bundles of freshly made pasta. These gourmet goodies make for wonderful food-related gifts.

Locally made crafts:

Additionally, Cortona is renowned for its traditional textiles, metalwork, and craftsmanship. Think about purchasing hand-carved wooden objects, one-of-a-kind jewelry, or woven textiles like scarves or table runners to bring home. These handcrafted items highlight the local talent and serve as treasured souvenirs.

Etruscan artifacts:

There might be miniature copies or replicas that draw inspiration from Etruscan artifacts because Cortona has a strong Etruscan past. These might be replicas made of porcelain, jewelry, or statues. You can establish a connection with the town's antiquity by owning a work of art with Etruscan influences.

Tuscan Recipe Book:

Bring a cookbook filled with dishes from Tuscany home. You'll be able to replicate the tastes of Cortona in your home kitchen. Identify books that showcase the local cuisine, ingredients, and culinary methods.

Photographs and Memories:

Last but not least, remember to take pictures to preserve the memories of your vacation to Cortona. Take lots of photos of the picturesque surroundings, important landmarks, and your experiences in the town. These pictures will serve as priceless recollections of your trip in Cortona.

Before completing your purchases, don't forget to verify the rules of customs and the limitations of the airlines on the shipping of specific commodities, such as liquids or food products. Enjoy the process of choosing these special mementos because they will not only help you remember your vacation to Cortona, but they will also enable you to share a piece of this charming Italian town with your loved ones.

CONCLUSION

Cortona offers a lovely fusion of culture, the arts, the outdoors, and gracious hospitality. Everyone may find something to enjoy in Cortona, whether they are history buffs, art connoisseurs, foodies, or just looking for a peaceful getaway.

Explore Cortona's quaint alleyways, stop by historic locations like the imposing Medici Fortress and the Etruscan Museum, and take in the breath-taking views from the town's medieval walls to fully immerse yourself in the town's rich history. Explore Cortona's art galleries to learn more about its rich artistic history and to admire works by well-known regional and international masters.

Enjoy dishes prepared with fresh, regional ingredients in the town's restaurants, trattorias, and cafes to indulge in the mouthwatering flavors of Tuscan cuisine. A glass of superb local wine will be served together with regional specialties like homemade pasta, truffles, and Chianina meat, so don't miss out on this chance to try them.

Exploring the neighboring countryside's undulating hills, vineyards, and olive groves is a great activity for nature enthusiasts. Visit picturesque pathways for leisurely strolls or bike rides as you explore the splendor of the Tuscan countryside at your own speed. And Cortona provides a variety of spas, thermal baths, and wellness retreats where you may relax and regenerate.

Your visit to Cortona is enhanced by the city's yearly celebrations and activities. From the Archidado Joust to the Cortona Mix Festival, you'll have the chance to get to know the people and their way of life while taking in live music, art exhibits, and delectable cuisine.

When making travel arrangements to Cortona, make sure to take into account relevant details including lodging choices, modes of transportation, safety advice, and regional traditions. Learn some basic Italian words, become familiar with the customs of the area, and interact with the welcoming residents who will be delighted to share their passion for their community.

A trip to Cortona will leave you with lifelong memories. It offers an amazing experience thanks to its timeless beauty, rich cultural heritage, and friendly atmosphere. Cortona will capture your heart and entice you to come back often whether you're meandering through its cobblestone alleys, indulging in the tastes of Tuscany, or appreciating the panoramic views from its hilltops.

Pack your luggage, give in to Cortona's attraction, and set out on an adventure that will inspire, delight, and give you memories to treasure forever.

Recommendation

Take the opportunity to stroll through the historic heart of Cortona's streets and alleys while you explore the area. Explore its quaint squares, secret nooks, and historic structures. For further information on the town's rich past, don't forget to check out the spectacular Duomo and the Etruscan Museum.

Reach the Medici Fortress, climb:

- Enjoy sweeping views of the town and the surrounding countryside by climbing to the top of the Medici Fortress. It's a gratifying experience that offers calm and breath-taking views.

Lake Trasimeno excursion:

- Visit the adjacent Lake Trasimeno, Italy's fourth-largest lake, for the day. Swim or have a swim there, or rent a boat and explore the lovely islands. Don't pass up the chance to indulge in lakeside restaurants' fresh seafood specialties.

Investigate the Tuscan countryside:

- To discover the gorgeous Tuscan countryside surrounding Cortona, rent a car or take a trip. Visit the olive fields, vineyards, and quaint towns like Montepulciano and Pienza. Enjoy the world-famous cheeses and wines of the area while soaking in the breath-inspiring scenery.

Attend local events and festivals:

- If there are any festivals or events scheduled during your visit, check the local calendar. A few examples of Cortona's thriving cultural scene include the Archidado Joust, Cortona Mix event, and Cortona on the Move photography event.

Enroll in a Cooking Class:

- Attend a cooking class to discover the authentic tastes of Tuscany. Discover the techniques for making classic foods like homemade pasta, bruschetta, and tiramisu. Engage with regional cooks to learn the secrets of Tuscan cooking.

Wine tasting is fun:

- World-class wines are well known for coming from Tuscany. Wine tasting sessions can be had at nearby vineyards and wineries. Discover the process of making wine, try various types, and buy your favorite bottles to take home as a memento.

Engage the Community:

- Get to know the welcoming residents to learn more about Cortona's customs and culture. Visit the neighborhood markets, make friends in the cafes, and don't be afraid to seek advice or recommendations. Cortona locals are renowned for their cordial welcome.

Go for Long Walks:

- The best way to see Cortona is on foot. Enjoy leisurely strolls through its quaint streets while taking in the architecture, the striking colors, and the breathtaking scenery. Remember to put in comfortable shoes because parts of the streets may have incline and have cobblestones.

Adopt a Slow Pace:

- In Cortona, you may take your time and appreciate each minute. Spend some time relaxing on a piazza, eating a leisurely lunch, or just taking it all in. Immerse yourself in the community's easygoing way of life.

Cortona should not be rushed; it is a destination to be experienced. Allow yourself to be mesmerized by its beauty, to learn about its history, to savor its cuisine, and to bask in the friendliness of its people. You'll make lifelong memories in this alluring Italian town by heeding these suggestions.

Made in the USA
Monee, IL
07 February 2024

53106411R00134